MW01070205

THE
ADJACENT

EVOLVE YOUR ART

POSSIBLE

FROM BLANK CANVAS TO PROLIFIC ARTIST

NANCY HILLIS, M.D.

First published by The Artist's Journey Press 2021

Copyright © 2021 by Nancy Hillis, M.D.

Visit the author's website at https://artistsjourney.com

All rights reserved. No part of this publication may be reproduced, stored, distributed, or transmitted in any form or by any means, including electronic, mechanical, photocopying, recording, scanning, mechanical methods, or otherwise, except as permitted under Section 107 or 108 of the 1976 United States Copyright Act, without the prior written permission of the author. It is illegal to copy this book, post it to a website, or distribute it by any other means without permission. Requests to the author and publisher for permission should be addressed to the following email: support@nancyhillis.com.

Cover design and formatting by David Provolo
Edited by Bruce Sawhill, Ph.D.

First edition
ISBN: 978-1-955028-03-5

To Bruce

Whose soaring mind

and beautiful heart

transport me to the art

of the adjacent possible.

Table of Contents

Foreword 6

Preface 7

1. The Paradox .11

2. Journey Into the Unknown: Unfolding Possibility 18

3. The Inner Journey Is a Hero's Journey 22

4. The Essence of Creativity 44

5. The Inner Landscape 53

6. Cultivating Surprise 71

7. Phase Transitions & Creativity 81

8. Zero to One: You Can Start Anywhere 87

9. Experimentation & The Surprise Benefits of Ugly Art . . 96

10. The Paradoxical Freedom of Constraint 105

11. Creative Evolution & The Adjacent Possible 120

12. Three Tips for Artists 130

13. Three Massive Mistakes Even the Pros Make 135

14. Four Traps Artists Face 164

15. Three Invisible Paradoxes 187

16. The Adjacent Possible Creativity Challenge 213

Epilogue 218

Postscript 224

About the Author 225

Other Books by Nancy Hillis, M.D. 226

Forward

A Special Invitation (*The Artist's Journey Community*)

Join the "Adjacents", a group of wildly experimental artists in *The Artist's Journey* Community to connect, discuss the book and explore the adjacent possible in your art and life.

Go to www.artistsjourney.com/TAPBook and you'll see the link to join our community of artists.

Preface

My life's dream is to help people believe in themselves and especially in their creative process as artists.

The big idea of this small book is called **the adjacent possible**. It addresses the science of creativity and provides a map for continually evolving your art. It is a theoretical structure built to explain how Nature creates that is relevant to understanding how people create.

The art of activating the canvas and bringing a painting to life with your own personal language of mark-making, expressive gestures, and brushwork is nothing short of miraculous. To create authentic and alive art that is unique to you and your own vision is the ultimate attainment for an artist and yet, the most elusive.

Working with artists in classes over the years, I've observed overarching patterns in the life cycle of being an artist that profoundly affect ones' creative journey. **There is a crucial progression from going beyond emulating others, to moving past emulating yourself, to finally expressing your own unique art- art that is continually evolving.**

In this book, you will discover the groundbreaking concept from evolutionary biology and theoretical physics, the adjacent possible, that will transform your experience of creating art.

As you apply **the adjacent possible** to your art as well as your own personal life, you will also learn to nurture your creative process.

Being an artist is about continually evolving your art. It's a journey of cultivating your fullest self-expression and getting to the elusive deepest work your heart yearns to create.

Every brushstroke, every decision in your art, creates a set of possible paths that were not only invisible before, but didn't exist before you made that creative move. This is the adjacent possible.

In this book you'll learn to use the science of creativity, the adjacent possible, to deepen your artistic expression. You'll be guided to evolve your art, nudged to create art that surprises you and inspired to move past emulating not only others, but yourself in your art.

Becoming a great artist is about the movement of coming closer to who you are and reaching the fullest expression of YOU in your art.

With one foot in the known and one foot in the unknown, you'll become aware of your creative edge where the adjacent possible lives.

At the pivot point between creation and dissolution, you'll experience a state of poised instability. This is the art and science of the possible- a world of continuous creation.

I invite you to say yes to your creativity and to feel the potential you have inside yourself.

By listening to your creative impulse, you'll bring visibility to the invisible and allow nascent ideas from your unconscious to bubble up to the surface.

You have something inside that is calling you to express yourself. Say yes to your dreams and feel confident in your ability to do what you came here to do, despite self-doubt.

My passion is to guide you to believe in yourself so you can express your deepest art and live your most meaningful life. This is much of the reason why I became an existential psychiatrist and artist.

What is the dream that calls you? Will you say yes to your dream?

Your mission should you choose to accept it is to come with me on this inner journey, access the adjacent possible and create art you love. By the end of this book, you will be able to not only experiment in your art, but evolve your art.

Thank you for coming along with me on this journey.

Let's begin.

— **Nancy Hillis**

1. The Paradox

An Artist's Trajectory

Consider an artist, we'll call her Grace, toiling in obscurity for fifteen years whose fate changed in a matter of weeks. A friend invited her to submit two paintings for possible inclusion in a local museum exhibition.

While Grace didn't often exhibit her work, she had recently experienced a breakthrough in her art, an exhilarating feeling like teetering on a razor's edge between creation and collapse. Somehow, her experimental paintings held together when they hadn't before. Exploring edges and unexpected intersections of lines, she reveled in the contrasts of gritty and smooth, ugly and luscious, in the marks and fields of color that emerged.

A little voice inside her head said, *why not submit these new works for the upcoming museum show?*

Three months later, to her great surprise, two of her paintings were selected for the exhibition. By this time, she had almost forgotten she had applied.

She delivered the paintings by strapping them to the roof of her trusty old Honda, wrapped in plastic, because they were too big to fit inside.

Grace's Big Break

Later, arriving at the opening, she was speechless when she saw her two large paintings prominently displayed, one with a *Best of Show* ribbon hanging beside it.

A San Francisco art critic lauded her work in the local paper ahead of the show, calling it *edgy, revolutionary, a cross between Brice Marden and Joan Mitchell.*

Word got out. The room was buzzing like an artistic bee colony awaiting their queen. A *murmurage* swept across the space as her heels clicked through the doorway. Artists and collectors jockeyed for position; champagne glasses held at chest height serving as defensive weaponry. A superficially polite artistic scrum.

As she made her way to her painting, her friend whispered, *do you know who that man is? He's the art critic for the San Francisco Comical. He's friends with the museum curator.*

After the opening, invitations arrived for solo exhibitions in museums across the country. To Grace's delight, she was able to retire her Honda and drop the two part-time jobs she was holding down to keep the lights on.

Two years later, her big break came when a gallery in New York known for rejecting artists without an MFA from Yale or Columbia offered Grace a one woman show. She couldn't say no.

The New York Opening

In the velvet plushness of the air-conditioned classic old Manhattan hotel, sweat soaked her taffeta dress as she stepped into beige six-inch heels. A chill coursed through her body as her jaw locked up and her teeth chattered uncontrollably. *How was she going to speak?*

She had imagined this moment for years but dismissed it as a paint thinner induced fantasy. Perhaps the aromatic hydrocarbons had addled her brain. It was an improbable dream. *Would she blow it with self-conscious awkwardness?*

But something else bothered her.

In the whirlwind three years after the museum show in San Francisco, punctuated with shows and interviews, and despite her new-found popularity and financial security, a growing sense of vulnerability and dread had crept over her.

She felt exposed. She'd dreamt of being a celebrated artist, yet the reality terrified her. *What if they change their mind about my art?*

In her studio, she'd stare at her prize paintings and wonder how she could create more paintings like those. *Were these winners a fluke? Can I keep this up?*

Afraid to make a move lest she ruin a painting or worse, create something mediocre, she waited, hoping for inspiration, desperate for a solution.

She shivered as she recalled the frenzied months of creating the first twenty-four of twenty-five paintings that would hang in the New York show. A few months prior, Cannus O'Carolan, an Irish art critic, wrote a blistering review of her last exhibition, calling it derivative and pedestrian.

She dreaded his criticism. He was the tail that wagged the dog of the art world, feared by artistic pedestrians.

Struggling to create the series of paintings for the show, she tried to push her art further, to experiment, but ended up taking only minor risks and merely slightly varying each subsequent painting. Her seminal painting from three years prior kept getting in the way-as if it were a paint-by-number template tattooed on her retina. A plan doggedly followed.

Cannus was right. She had repeated herself.

She had two weeks left and one painting to complete before shipping the new series to New York, this time not upon her Honda's roof.

Reviewing the first twenty-four paintings, she felt humiliated. She yearned to disappear, to run back to the time before anyone knew her work, but it was too late. Cannus would likely be at the show. It would be a disaster.

She slept fitfully. A crying newborn appeared in her dreamworld studio, and she awoke, startled by the image. She needed to do something new, something radical.

What have I got to lose? Even an ugly painting is better than a predictable one.

She loaded her number eight *Escoda* sash brush with black latex house paint and lost all sense of time.

A Hotel Room
In New York

In the hotel room in New York, reaching for Xanax, she spilled the bottle.

Her contacts not yet in, eyes too myopic to find her glasses, she raked the carpet with her fingers. Like her mother and grandmother, she carried the lineage of blind artists dotting her family tree like blurry leaves.

Her heartbeat throbbed in her ears as the room's walls closed in.

She found the cool, hard pill near her feet and gulped it. The exhibition was starting in an hour. *Would Cannus be there?*

The Exhibition

The opening had been underway for a half hour when she arrived, breathless from the taxi. She'd spilled chamomile tea on her skirt but folded the voluminous material to hide the stain.

The tapping of her stilettos as she walked in on wobbly toothpick legs made her self-conscious. *Why had she not bought the $900 designer shoes instead of the $100 ones?*

As she teetered into the show, she saw a crowd gathered around a painting in the anteroom of the gallery. It was her last painting of the series, the one she had just finished.

The room grew louder, fueled by banality and champagne. Cannus held court as he discussed the painting in his inimitable gruff voice. A leather-lunged bellower, his words carried across the room as he gesticulated animatedly. Grace's throat tightened as she neared the group.

Creating that last painting was exhilarating, it was completely different from the first 24. What did Cannus think of it?

As she approached, Cannus turned towards her. His eyes squinted with a quizzical expression. The room fell silent. Her raspy breath deafening to her ears.

Bracing herself, she imagined he would say something like: *Here's Miss flash-in-the-pan* because Cannus was known for barking at artists both in person and in writing.

What he said instead was:

Did you actually paint this?

2. Journey into The Unknown: Unfolding Possibility

A great flame follows a little spark.
— Dante Alighieri

Sometimes you need to see your work with fresh eyes. Like the artist in Chapter One realizing she was emulating herself by trying to replicate her award-winning painting. Only then could she break through her cycle of repetition.

As artists, we live on the edge of another reality, and that reality is just a decision away.

The more creative we are, the more choices we open up for ourselves to decide between, and thus the more possibilities we gain access to.

This new set of possibilities is **the adjacent possible**, and it is the key to living a creative life.

Creativity is about being open to accessing the mystery of surprises of your unknown potential and incorporating that newness into your existing life, coming to terms with the contrast and disjuncture.

Life is about continually exploring the mystery of the **adjacent possible**, not solving it. Life is not solvable in a conventional static sense because it is perpetually incomplete, and its incompleteness pulls us forward.

By making room for surprise, you build your sense of self trust, develop and refine your instinct, and find comfort in the questions instead of simply seeking answers.

An Old Idea in a New Context

Many revolutions are old ideas in new contexts, new combinations.

This book is about bringing an older idea from evolutionary biology, the adjacent possible, to a new context: creativity. The adjacent possible itself has even older roots in the variation and selection associated with evolutionary processes.

Life is about continually pursuing the mystery of the adjacent possible, not solving it.

Aliveness is about accessing the mysterious, and this idea is about thriving in the questions instead of settling for answers that become transitory and irrelevant.

The adjacent possible is another way to understand embracing surprise and stepping into the unknown. This idea taps into something vital that is not being seen or heard. It brings visibility to the invisible.

The Implications for Your Life

Creativity relies upon the constraint of decision.

It is the miracle of saying yes, and it is the moment you bring something to life. The moment you say yes, the moment you begin anything, you bring it into being. The door swings open, and anything can happen.

Constraints are vital to creation. In making creative decisions, you cause other possibilities to fall away.

You must eliminate some of the old to open to something new.

Constraint & Specificity

Constraint and specificity are essential to creativity.

All visual patterns seen together create visual mud. All sounds heard together add up to auditory static. This is not compelling art, except perhaps to make a point.

Art Depends Upon Decision

Creativity, uniqueness, and choice intersect and connect.

It is all connected. Your choices carve out your identity on your journey of self-expression and this relies upon trusting yourself. You are the sum of many choices, conscious and unconscious.

This is navigating the landscape of believing in what you have inside of you that only you can express. It is also believing there are paths that will open for you. You may not see them yet, but they are waiting for you and will unfold.

3. The Inner Journey Is a Hero's Journey

Our lives are a hero's journey of moving from the known to the unknown and returning, transformed.

As artists, we continually step into the unknown and evolve our work. We search and find our way, lose and find ourselves in our paintings and explore and experiment on our journey of self-expression.

I'm reminded of the writings of Dante Alighieri (1265 - 1321) who, in his literary masterpiece, *The Divine Comedy*, embarked on a perilous journey to find meaning in his search for divine love, for himself, for God. Likewise, as artists, we too are on our own journey of meaning, aliveness, and transformation.

In the opening salvo, Dante wrote:

> *In the middle of the road of my life*
> *I awoke in a dark wood*
> *Where the true way was wholly lost*

The Human Condition

Opening the story with a crisis, a tried-and-true plot technique, Dante takes us immediately into the human condition, into the existential issues of being alive and yet feeling lost, unsure, and alone.

We're compelled to venture forth into the *terra incognita*, the territory of *not knowing*. We are called to adventure.

We're invited to investigate and reflect on the great mystery of our heart and its desires, to explore the reaches of our imagination, to examine our resistances and blocks and whatever holds us back.

And it turns out there are guides to help us through the perils and frustrations. Dante was guided through hell by the great Roman poet Virgil. We have our own guides: mentors, teachers, and other artists.

The Dark Night of The Soul

Eventually, you encounter the mother of all perils: the *dark night of the soul*. This is the moment of greatest self-doubt when you must face yourself. This is the moment when you feel like giving up.

As you wrestle down the dark angels of despair, this is the time pregnant with possibility- the possibility of self-transformation.

This is the lowest point, the nadir, and yet the place where the most profound change and revelation occurs.

Transformation

And ultimately, you are transformed in some way.

This transformation is about trusting yourself, even if only a little more than before. It takes the form of going deeper as you express your feelings and truth in your art.

Return

And finally, you return to your life, transformed, carrying new knowledge and confidence - but never quite the same after your awakening.

The Call

And then, another dream calls you- and you say "yes" and are immediately plunged into the unknown and the cycle continues throughout your life.

The hero's journey is when you finally say yes to the call, when you refuse the refusal. It does not have to involve swords and armies and conquest that often accompany mythology. Those things are merely props on the most important journey of all, your inner journey.

Yearning for Self-Expression

I was thinking about the hero's journey when an artist wrote to me about noticing the barriers, she creates for herself and the self-doubt that holds her back in her art. Her previous working method was no longer satisfying, and she wanted to explore something new.

She yearned for something more.

Yet, as she dipped her toe into the waters of acrylic paint, she felt tentative, apprehensive, and uncertain.

Let's Delve Deeper into The Hero's Journey

Many people know that Joseph Campbell (1904 – 1987) popularized the idea of the hero's journey in 1949 in his book *The Hero with A Thousand Faces* but the concept was first conceived and formulated in 1871 by the English founder of the field of Cultural Anthropology, Edward Burnett Tylor (1832 – 1917).

Tylor discovered recurring patterns of deep psychological significance in plots of epic stories threading throughout history and across cultures.

Campbell was also influenced by the esteemed psychologist Carl Jung (1875 - 1961). A contemporary of Freud, Jung was interested in symbology, mythology, and the collective unconscious- the part of the unconscious mind derived from ancestral memory and experience and common to all humans.

Campbell was fascinated by the hero's call to adventure and the psychological implications as the hero is invited to move from ordinary life, *the known*, into an experience of the unknown.

The hero's journey has a general structure, a kind of script outline that occurs again and again. It goes like the following, starting at the top and proceeding clockwise.

The Call

Our lives are a hero's journey. We're continually going from the known to the unknown, accessing parts of ourselves that are ineffable, inarticulable and mysterious.

You're living your life; things are going fine except you notice you yearn for something. You want a feeling of aliveness, a sense of meaning. Something calls you. Maybe action. You want an adventure. You desire to try something, to learn something new.

But the problem is you're afraid.

Maybe you want to paint. Maybe you want to try something creative. Maybe you want to sing arias or perform in the orchestra. Perhaps you want to dance or choreograph. Or maybe you just want a feeling of aliveness- something that brings you alive.

The Refusal

But the problem is you say no. You refuse. You reject your dream.

You're on the edge, teetering towards something new. You want to say yes, but you're afraid. You tell yourself: *It's not practical. I'll get to it later.*

The problem with refusal is the pain of living a life of unlived dreams.

The danger in the refusal is you stay in the known rather than stepping into the unknown. The known is safe, familiar, and perhaps deadening. One way this manifests creatively is *you repeat yourself in your art.*

We saw this happen in the story of the artist in Chapter One. The tendency to emulate your successful artworks is a danger throughout your life cycle as an artist.

This is a kind of Faustian deal. The cost of creating safe art merely because it sells, is that your art no longer brings you alive. It has a stale, predictable quality.

The challenge is to fight the urge to repeat what works and to take risks, experiment and evolve as an artist.

Your eyes glaze over, your inner light dimmed by resignation, regret and a feeling of boredom and quiet despair. You imprison yourself in a house of meaninglessness like Bluebeard in his castle.

Joseph Campbell wrote:

Refusal of the summons converts the adventure into its

negative. Walled in boredom, hard work or culture, the subject loses the power of significant affirmative action and becomes a victim to be saved. His flowering world becomes a wasteland of dry stones, and his life feels meaningless.

Yet something tugs at you. Time is rushing by. You can't afford to wait. You doubt yourself. You consider saying yes, but still turn your face away.

This scenario plays out repetitively until you can take it no longer. You've simply had enough of saying no to yourself. Because if you do this enough, other people take the hint and start saying "no" to you also.

Crossing The Threshold

Your dream; however, will not be rejected so handily. The tension builds until you can no longer say no.

But then, there's an inciting incident. In literature, that's the moment when everything changes. Your life is never the same after this experience.

And it's at this moment that you say yes.

But there are perils. Immediately you must face the ups and downs. In literature, you're going along, things are going great, and you're hit again by another slap and then another.

And then, it gets even worse.

And you're immediately plunged into the unknown. Down, deep, into the unconscious. Down into the underbelly of the monster.

But guides show up- mentors, teachers, even friends who go on part of the journey with you. They help you cross the threshold, just as the great Roman poet Virgil aided Dante in his hour of need in the dark wood.

The Dark Night of The Soul

And then, it gets worse. Eventually you reach the moment that's akin to *the dark night of the soul*. It is when you must go inward and face yourself. This is the moment of greatest self-doubt when you feel like nothing's happening.

This is the moment when all feels lost. You ask yourself: *What was I thinking?*

Am I really an artist? Do I think I can sing opera? Or get this role? Write a book?

You might be in the middle of a painting, and you don't know what to do.

The Transformation

It's the moment when you feel like giving up. But it's also the moment of transformation.

It is the moment when you must go inward and face yourself. No one can do this for you. By facing the dark night of the soul, and there may be several, you begin to trust yourself and believe in yourself.

So, there's the transformation. It may be wisdom, intuition, the treasures of all that you learn on your adventures.

It's the moment of transformation when you grapple with the dark angels of despair and ultimately learn to trust yourself.

And in trusting yourself, you continue your artist's journey and begin to experiment and explore in a way that you haven't before. You begin to risk more, and you begin to trust that this is where the magic is.

The magic is in the *not knowing, the mystery*. If you follow your strategic mind, replicating what you already know, it won't feel alive.

The Return

And then, you bring those back with you. You come back to your life, different than before. Transformed, with the treasures, the understandings of yourself perhaps.

And you're back in your life, living your life. And then, you're called again because you want something else. This is a never-ending cycle. We're continually living the artist's journey, the hero's journey.

From The Known to The Unknown

The fundamental component of the hero's journey is the movement from the known to the unknown.

The Unknown is much of the journey. Like the proverbial iceberg, most of it is under water and not accessible without further effort.

The Hero's Journey in Different Creative Pursuits

THE HERO'S JOURNEY **IN ART**

DANTE ALLIGHIERI

The Hero's Journey in Art

The hero's journey in art begins when you want to do something new. You want something to emerge and evolve in your art, but you've got successful paintings that sell, or you create pretty paintings and you're afraid to change.

The danger as an artist is the tendency to stay in the refusal. When you play it safe, when you refuse the call of stepping into the unknown in your art, your paintings reflect your fear.

Repeating what has worked in the past is a deadening place for art. It might seem to work for a while, but eventually you lose heart because your art becomes static.

You must move past resistance and embrace the unknown. Don't cut a Faustian deal and repeat successful paintings. Create art that bring you alive by embracing exploration and experimentation.

The Hero's Journey in Literature & Film

We experience the hero's journey in the great stories like Dante's *Inferno*.

A classic example of the hero's journey in film is *Star Wars*. George Lucas met with Joseph Campbell and was strongly influenced by his work and the structure of the hero's journey.

The Call & The Refusal

Luke Skywalker, the hero, talks to Obi-Wan Kenobi, trainer of Jedi Knights, and encounters Princess Leia from the Rebel Alliance. Obi-Wan and Princess Leia are fighting against the evil empire, but Luke refuses the call even though he's asked twice.

The Inciting Incident

There is an inciting incident. This is the moment when everything changes, and Luke's life will never be the same.

Luke was living with his aunt and uncle until they were murdered by agents of the Empire. His father was presumably dead, we don't know at this point what fate befell him. *What will happen next?* There's a moment when Luke is compelled to say yes, but there are perils.

Luke views the remains of his aunt and uncle and decides in that moment to say yes to the call. It will not be an easy journey.

Luke agrees to travel with Obi-Wan Kenobi to Mos Eisele, cleverly disguised as Death Valley in California with some computational image enhancement. The viewpoint from where the "wretched hive of scum and villainy" is first observed is, perhaps not by chance, called *Dante's View in* real life

The Dark Night of The Soul

After Luke's commitment comes the dark night, the moment of the greatest self-doubt. All seems lost. It is the dark night of the soul because Luke feels completely alone.

The Death Star warship blows up Princess Leia's planet. This is the darkest moment and where the story turns. It can happen to the hero or the hero's friends and others. This is the moment of truth, to surrender or to fight.

When you face your darkest moments, your transformation, your greatest fears, there's a chance you can transform by going deeply inside yourself.

Luke's challenge is to destroy the Death Star battleship. His mentors and compatriots join in his mission, vastly outnumbered but with secret and powerful knowledge obtained with help from colleagues who have joined his mission.

Transformation

At the height of the battle, Luke must go inward and let go. He deactivates the guidance computer of his little fighter spacecraft, and he goes inward and trusts himself. In the movie, this is called "Using the Force," but I suspect this is a way of giving a name to the creative energy within that drives us forward and weaves meaning out of our lives.

Luke was fighting for something bigger than himself, good versus evil. He blew up the Death Star only by trusting himself.

A Hero's Return

He returned to his life, transformed - to inner trust, wisdom and understanding and to a hero's welcome.

The Hero's Journey in Music

The hero's journey can be involved in something abstract, something beyond characters such as in music.

Here's something to think about: Imagine the hero is not a character but a theme or a melody.

An excellent example is Beethoven's *Fifth Symphony*.

The Hero's Journey In Music

Returns to itself

Individual Character; Signature

Reasserts its individuality

Undergoes a test

Bent, Kneaded, Twisted, Pushed

Thrown into minor keys, different harmonies

Distorted, modified, reflected

The melody goes on a journey, just like the hero, proceeding clockwise in the diagram above.

It has an individual character and signature, a theme or melody. We all know the four-note theme of Beethoven's *Fifth Symphony*.

It undergoes a test.

It's distorted, modified, reflected.

It's thrown into other keys and harmonies.

It gets bent, kneaded, twisted, pushed.

It reasserts its individuality and then triumphantly returns to itself, but ever so much more so- its very own hero's journey.

The Hero's Journey in Childhood Play

We see the hero's journey in childhood's play as children explore heroic themes.

THE
HERO'S
JOURNEY **HIDE AND SEEK**

PEEK A BOO

We see this when we look at childhood games such as *Hide and Seek* and *Peek a Boo*, games about losing and finding yourself, and being re-found and re-asserting yourself. It's about being mirrored and reflected in your mother's or father's eyes and experiencing yourself.

Heinz Kohut (1913 – 1981) was an eminent psychologist who talked about the game of *This Little Piggy* as a kind of falling apart and coming back together again.

This little piggy goes to the market, this little piggy stays home, this little piggy had roast beef, this little piggy had none, this little piggy said wee, wee, wee all the way home

Children play this game over and over. Each little piggy does different things, has different journeys and the last one returns home, symbolizing return, a form of coming back to yourself.

The Hero's Journey: Finding Yourself

The Hero's Journey is about rediscovering and affirming yourself in your art and life. It's about finding yourself again, and again.

In the hero's journey you rediscover and affirm yourself.

You move from the known to the unknown, facing your fears as you undergo challenges and tests, searching and finding your way, being helped by guides, and ultimately facing yourself in the *dark night of the soul* which is the moment of greatest self-doubt yet also the moment of transformation.

Something New Is Calling You

In your art and life, something new, something ineffable, unknown and inarticulable is calling you. Something nascent, in seed form, is trying to emerge and be expressed.

Even so, you feel hesitant.

This is to be expected. It's scary to step deeper into *not knowing,* to wrestle down the dark angels of self-doubt, to face some of the works that emerge from this exploration, many of which feel unfamiliar, strange, unrecognizable, even "ugly."

The fundamental component of the hero's journey is this movement of saying yes to what calls you and plunging into the unknown.

Like exploring the Minotaur's cave, you follow the string back to return to the known world and when you see the light, you begin looking around for the next unknown.

This is a recurring, spiraling cycle in your life cycle as an artist.

The Adjacent Possible & The Unknown Unknown

In the case of the adjacent possible, which we explore throughout this book, we take this cycle a step further. With one foot in the known and one foot in the unknown, we access the *unknown unknown*.

The unknown unknown is the set of things you don't know that you don't know. It is the root of true surprise.

After we face the unknown unknown, we return through the Minotaur's labyrinth to the known again, in a looping, continuous spiral, expanding the territory of the known a little bit each time.

Like dikes in Holland that encircle a small amount of sea and gradually transform it into land, the creative life involves carving new bits of unknown out of the universe and incorporating them into the known.

As a creative, you are continually tapping into the unknown.

Give yourself permission to allow this deep experimentation that is pushing for expression. Show up in your studio without knowing what is going to happen. See it as a process of curiosity and inquiry. Create exploratory studies and experimental works without worrying about outcome.

Full Circle

We return full circle to Dante Alighieri, who stepped into the unknown and found himself in the dark wood, lost, but guided by Virgil.

The hero's journey is about rediscovering yourself and affirming yourself in your art and life. It's about finding yourself, again and again.

Reflect on all the hero's journeys you have experienced. All the moments when you said yes to something you dreamed of, something you wanted to try, perhaps it was an adventure, something that scared you, something where you said to yourself: *I don't know what I'm doing*, but somehow you went ahead anyway.

4. The Essence of Creativity

The hero's journey, luckiness, the adjacent possible and the mathematical concept of zero to one show up in surprising ways in art, life, and creativity. We assemble the cast of characters.

Prelude To a Heroic Journey

Dr. Bruce Sawhill, my partner, had an astonishing experience that combined the hero's journey, the adjacent possible and the concept of zero to one while swimming in the Pacific Ocean in Santa Cruz, California.

This is not just any swimming. It is more like full immersion baptism in the cold Pacific waters of northern California in November without a wetsuit.

He thinks this is fun.

Bruce is a Stanford educated theoretical physicist, mathematician and complexity scientist who finds swimming conducive to pondering the mysteries of the universe. It is prayer and sensory deprivation - alone with wind, wave, and breath.

Perhaps the frigid water (54 degrees F, 12 degrees C) brings his brain closer to absolute zero and the beginnings of superconductivity.

Maybe the prone swimming position is important. I like to think it allows increased blood perfusion to the area of his brain where his most treasured ideas are kept.

Bruce is aware of my fascination with the hero's journey as a paradigm for many of life's deepest challenges and mysteries.

He had a remarkable encounter while swimming he told me about after returning home and running all the hot water out of the shower.

Bruce's Story

I was cruising along in shallow water near the shore because there are no lifeguards on duty, and this is great white shark season.

I know you are fascinated by the hero's journey, and it occurred to me that every open-water swim is a kind of hero's journey in miniature. But this one was different.

Here is how my Hero's Journey went through the milestones of Joseph Campbell's mapping in less than an hour:

The call: *It is a good day for a swim. The sky is blue. Birds are singing.*

The refusal: *It is windy. It is cold. It's November. What was I thinking? The water is murky. I heard someone saw a shark somewhere. I will go tomorrow.*

Saying yes: Taking the plunge: *Literal, no explanation necessary.*

The dark night of the soul: *I am a half mile from the stairs at the shore and I am getting cold and tired.*

The reaching within and digging down deep: *Pushing hard, getting slapped around by waves, taking great breaths, heart pumping fiercely to counter the unforgiving and relentless cold assault from outside.*

The reward: *Climbing out, feeling more alive than seems humanly possible.*

Finally,

The Return: *a hot shower followed by a frothing quaff of ice-cold beer in a heavy frosted mug followed by a dreamless nap of the blessed.*

As I was in the reaching within part of the journey, the beautiful ripples fascinated me on the sandy bottom as my shadow passed over them, my hands throwing whirling vortices of bubbles.

Just then, something moving and white caught my attention out of the corner of my eye.

It was not a **great white** kind of white; it was more like a plant, anchored to the bottom, waving its tendrils in the currents.

I changed course and stroked over to the mysterious organism. It seemed odd that a plant would flourish in a great expanse of barren sand.

It took a moment to overcome the cognitive dissonance and recognize the object for what it was.

I couldn't believe what my eyes revealed.

It was a book.

I dove and picked up the hardback. It had not been there long. It did not dissolve in my fingers. I leafed through the sodden mass to find a title page.

It was Spartacus, by Ben Kane. The story of a hero's journey if ever there was one.

I am not necessarily a disciple of the idea that the Universe sends you what you need, but like the pioneering Danish quantum physicist Niels Bohr who kept a good luck horseshoe above his office door said: You know, my friends tell me it works whether you believe in it or not.

I have been swimming in these waters for many years and have seen very few books on the ocean floor.

In fact, this was zero to one.

Having nowhere to put the book (I was wearing a Speedo) and rapidly getting chilled, I released the tome to the waters and watched it flutter its storied pages on its slow-motion descent, settling on the bottom with a little puff of sand.

It seemed like a dream.

And then I returned - back to my life.

I swam back to the stairs, climbed out, and cycled home, elated by this auspicious message from Poseidon.

I could not wait to tell Nancy

The story of the book submerged in the waters of the Pacific

The Connection Between the Hero's Journey & The Adjacent Possible

Ocean is not only an exercise in thinking about the Hero's Journey, and by extension, the Artist's Journey, but also about the Adjacent Possible.

Bruce did not go on a swim to find a book, but it happened anyway. He did not even think he might find a book. It was truly an unknown unknown.

It was because he was open to explore the unknown that he literally *changed his course* to go look at the mysterious object on the bottom of the sea floor, which turned out to be a book.

Luckiness

Researchers who study the phenomenon of *luckiness* have discovered two personal habits highly correlated with people who consider themselves lucky.

The first habit is that they change up their daily routines. They do not take the same route to work every day, paint with the same palette or tools every day, or only talk to the same group of people every day.

The second habit is they avoid over-scheduling. They leave breathing space in their day for reflection and replenishment.

Making Room
for Surprise

And finally, and perhaps most importantly, they make room for surprise.

HABITS

That correlate with luckiness

- Change your daily routines
- Avoid overscheduling
- Make room for surprise

What use is an Adjacent Possible of surprise, learning, and wonder if there is no time to take advantage of it?

You must cultivate an attitude of being surprisable.

This applies particularly to artists.

The Art of The Possible

What if a universe of possibilities is always there, and all we must do is open our eyes and hearts to allow it in?

We're swimming in an ocean of possibilities and mostly unaware of it.

Men occasionally stumble over the truth.
But most of them pick themselves up and hurry off
As if nothing had happened.
—Winston Churchill

The Adjacent Possible & Creativity

For something to be born, something else must pass away. This is the life/death/life cycle we see in nature.

Creativity is about *decision*, from the Latin *decidire*, meaning to cut away.

The adjacent possible is the notion that at any moment there is a spider-web of possible paths leading away from where one stands, and the action of taking each step creates a new set of paths.

Awareness of this ever-renewing world of possibilities is the key to creativity.

We are continuously writing and rewriting our narratives.

Reality is slippery and diaphanous, despite impressions of solidity and permanence. Given this shifting reality, it is important to keep track of where you have been.

In Greek mythology, Theseus in the labyrinth of the Minotaur brought along a ball of thread to map his steps so he could live to tell his story of victory.

To explore the labyrinth of the adjacent possible requires a cutting away, a removal of past encumbrances, a cleaning off the mud of ones' existential boots to walk on fresh paths more easily.

This is the task that awaits you as an artist and creative, should you accept it.

5. The Inner Landscape

In the beginner's mind there are many possibilities,
but in the expert's, there are few.

-Shunryu Suzuki

Cultivating an open mind and maintaining the teachable spirit of a beginner is a potent practice for artists at every stage of development.

Being An Artist Is About 'Not Knowing'

One thing I have learned on this journey is that being an artist is about continually growing. It is about searching and finding your way as you create. It is about *experimentation*.

Artists are continually stepping into the unknown and seeing what bubbles up from the unconscious.

As an artist, you are facing the perils of creating daily:

- self-doubt

- vulnerability

- inner criticism

- second guessing

- overthinking

- procrastination

- and many more

As an artist, you know you must face the dark night of the soul of self-doubt every time you step into your studio. You understand that cultivating an attitude of experimentation is vital to your development.

You know that to create your deepest work you must take risks, to paint an *ugly* painting, to write the messy first draft, to explore unfamiliar sequences of moves in your choreography.

These *ugly* works are vital to your development as an artist and yet the tendency is to fall back into patterns that have worked before.

We know that as artists we must keep pushing the envelope, searching, and experimenting to develop and create works that astonish us.

Yet we can easily devolve into repeating our successful paintings, compositions, and stories.

Copying Yourself

There is a danger of copying yourself. We keep doing what we have done before because it worked or garnered approval.

We want to create successful art.

The path with the grooved ruts is familiar and we fear branching off into unknown territory lest we get lost and our paintings, our manuscript, our choreographed dance becomes an ugly, chaotic mess.

The underbelly of creating art you love is you might fear that your next work will not live up to these successful and illustrious ones.

I think this is especially true when you have received critical acclaim or sold out most of your show or even when friends like your work.

You play it safe and stay within the bounds of the familiar. Before you know it you are creating the next artwork in a way that is barely distinguishable from the last one.

The Risks of Copying Yourself

You can become stuck in a place of trying to recreate what has previously worked in your art as well as other artists' work.

We go through a life cycle as artists where we feel inspired by other artist's work and try to create something like that, but ultimately this feels derivative or flat. We end up feeling ungratified and bored.

The *problem* is you want to create and share art that is uniquely yours. You want to feel like a real artist where your work comes from **inside** of you, from your own source. The *challenge* is you are not sure how to do that.

We can talk about exploration, experimentation, and shaking things up to get out of your rut, *but the underlying issue that affects everything is your inner landscape, your mindset, your psychology, your relationship to yourself.*

The Inner Shift

There is an inner shift that is essential for creating deep and personal art. This mindset shift is the thing that will open experimentation, exploration, playfulness, risk taking, searching, and finding your way as you create and allowing yourself to step into a place of *not knowing*.

It will access a state of wonder. It will help you create raw, spontaneous, and intuitive work that delights and astonishes you.

It will open channels of creativity and guide you to developing your work by allowing your expression to come through, including the "ugly" work.

It will teach you to value your work, even the orphaned pieces that are unfamiliar or uncomfortable.

The Holy Grail

What is this one inner shift? What is this holy grail?

The holy grail is trusting yourself. This is where your deepest work comes from. This is the most important mindset shift that will affect not just your art but your life.

This is the secret to creating your most personal and authentic art.

The Advantages of Obscurity

What is the advantage of not being well known?

There is an interesting story and book, *Women of Abstract Expressionism*, from the Denver Art Museum exhibit on women abstract expressionists. This was a group of women in the San Francisco Bay Area in the avant-garde milieu of the late 1940s and early 1950s who were exploring abstract expressionist art, and they were not famous.

They found **there was an advantage to not having the light shining on them.** They felt free to experiment. They were not so afraid because there were no critical eyes staring at them. *Is someone looking at my art? Is someone criticizing me?*

There is power, paradoxically, in obscurity.

When you break out of obscurity, it can feel threatening. This is when you must learn to validate and hold onto yourself.

Here are some questions for you:

- What would you create if you were invisible?

- How would you sing if no one were watching?

- What if you were unself-conscious in your art making?

- What risks would you take if the outcome didn't matter?

Imagine bringing this freedom of expression into the arena when you **are** being seen.

You can continue to take those risks and stand firmly in yourself, even though some people will not like your creations.

Facing Rejection & Criticism

This brings up questions of:

- How do you face rejection?

- How do you handle negative comments?

- How do you manage criticism and the self-talk that may come after these experiences?

Inevitably, someone will say something negative about you and your art.

The genuine issue happens inside of you.

It is never pleasant when someone is critical of your art. The worst part: however, is **when a part of you agrees with the criticism.**

A part of you concurs with the negative assessment of your art, but another part of you says: *No, no, no* in response to the outer and inner criticism.

This is an internal struggle.

The issue is inner criticism. Inner criticism can get activated by outer criticism. The worst criticism is inside, not outside.

Internal Versus External Validation: Prisoners of Praise

A pervasive issue for artists is looking for praise and recognition from their audience. They become prisoners of praise, reliant upon external validation for their sense of accomplishment and identity.

Relying upon approval from others takes you further away from yourself. You give your power away when you look outside yourself for validation.

Who you are is not contingent upon anyone else's opinion. You decide who you are. You are the author, artist, and composer of your life.

You were not born to please people. You came here to be yourself and continually grow as a person and artist.

When you understand that you are here to be yourself, you will see that someone else's negativity reflects them, their state of mind, not you.

Do not worry about what someone else is saying. They are living their life, and you are living yours. The more you show up in the world and increase your surface area with your art, the more you will face criticism. Be prepared to hold onto yourself when external criticism arises.

Trusting Yourself

Let's talk about trusting yourself, trusting the work you are developing, trusting your vision.

You may doubt yourself. You may wonder:

- *Do I have it?*

- *Am I talented enough?*

- *Is it too late?*

There is some beautiful work at Stanford by Carol Dweck on growth versus static mindset.

Static mindset says: *If I am already not good enough, the game is over.* It is as if there is a limited amount of possibility. It says: *Maybe I am not talented.* This mindset is sensitive to criticism and others' perceptions and assessments.

Growth mindset says: *I can learn this. I can continue to get better. I can grow and strengthen as an artist. It's okay if it's awkward right now and I don't like some of my paintings or my manuscript or how I performed at the audition.*

You will not like all your paintings, manuscripts, auditions, and performances. This is okay. It is great. Some of your greatest work will emerge out of mistakes, failures, and awkward moments.

Your Inner Narrative

The words you say to yourself matter. Speaking to yourself in an encouraging manner makes a difference.

For example, you could say:

- *Let's do this*

- *Let's go for it*

- *Let's explore what happens next*

You can adopt a way of talking to yourself that is not critical but is rather *a state of allowing* and giving yourself permission.

Speaking to yourself in this positive way feeds your trust in yourself and trusting yourself helps you to do this. It is a positive loop.

If you can embrace the *ugly* works, the mistakes, the so-called failures, you free yourself up to do anything you wish with your art.

Let that sink in.

When fear arises, you can mediate it with your attitude of embracing it. By embracing your fears of ruining it, of creating terrible, *ugly* work- there is something available to you- the willingness to go ahead, anyway. Things are not so fraught. You feel more confidence, a sense of aliveness.

You move away from the idea that your art defines you, but rather, you define it. You are the author of your art. You know there will inevitably be *ugly* works and you embrace these as essential and vital to your creative, exploratory, and experimental process.

Rather than a static thing, creating is a process. There will be failures as your journey unfolds. Not every work of art will work out.

Research by Nathan Kross, PhD. explores why your most important relationship is with your inner voice. Some of Kross' early work was on the effect of the inner dialogue when giving a public speech. The way people spoke to themselves made a big difference in how they performed.

If the speaker used a first-person personal pronoun such as "I", they did not do so well, for example, saying: *I'm not good at this. I don't know how this is going to go. I'm scared.*

Whereas people who spoke to themselves using second or third person pronouns performed better with their speeches.

For example, they would say things like:

- *Let's go do this.*

- *Hey, this will be fun.*

- *Kate, you've got this*

- *Let's go paint.*

- *Let's explore*

It is more helpful than getting trapped in the "I" which then implies one's sense of identity is at stake.

The Language of Comparison

We overvalue starting conditions. We think: *Where am I right now? Oh, I'm never going to be as great as that artist, who is already ahead of me.*

This is a bad idea. It is the language of comparison. There is no need to compare yourself to another because you can only do your own work and live your own life.

It is more important to know what you are going to be doing in the next year, the next 1000 plus days, the next 10 years to move forward. Do not overvalue the importance of where you are now but reflect on the direction in which you are going.

Notice the frequency of your practice of learning and keep going. Over time, you will grow as an artist, but you must **start**.

Believe In Yourself

Imagine believing in yourself and accessing a sense of playfulness and an attitude of allowing. Observe children. They continually explore and experiment. You have this playful nature in you as well. It is there; it is available, and it is about accessing and re-finding it and bringing it alive again.

My invitation is for you to say *yes* to exploration and experimentation in your art.

The biggest issue I see in every abstract painting course and workshop I teach is the difficulty artists have with trusting themselves.

Reflection: Bring Visibility to The Invisible

Write about your biggest takeaways from this lesson on the inner landscape.

What is coming up for you, as you read this chapter about:

- growth mindset versus static mindset

- the inner language, the kinds of things you are saying to yourself

- the inner landscape of creating your art

- believing in yourself as an artist

What are your observations, aha's, and revelations?

If you can bring visibility to the invisible, to what is going on in your inner dialogue with yourself, this will help you step back, gain insight and go ahead, anyway.

Exercise

The poet John Keats captured the essence of being an artist in these lines:

> *I am certain of nothing but the holiness of the heart's affections and the truth of the imagination.*
> —John Keats

What is in your imagination? What are your heart's affections? What dreams live inside you, waiting to be explored?

Write about your dreams — the ones that call you, yet you avoid because you fear failure, humiliation, or criticism.

Maybe you want to

- sing

- act

- write a play

- dance

- learn dressage

- play a musical instrument

- write a novel

- sew

- knit

- paint

- create a comedic routine

Whatever it is, write your dreams on the left-hand side of a sheet of paper.

On the right-hand side of the paper, write the things you say to yourself about your dreams. What are the thoughts that are stopping you? These could be your biggest fears about trying this new thing you are interested in. It could be an excuse. It could be your resistance.

Write quickly before you start second-guessing and backtracking. First impressions are important here.

When you're finished, take a crayon or marker and mark out, cover over or cross out what you wrote that is stopping you.

Cross out or color over all the excuses and resistances and replace them with a growth mindset mantra. Write words like: *We can do this, we've got this. Let's go. Let's try it out. Let's experiment.*

One of the most powerful things you can do is work with the words you say to yourself.

And you could say things such as

- *This is an exploratory work*

- *This is an experimental study*

- *It's all a work in progress*

- *Mistakes are beneficial*

- *It's great to create ugly artwork*

- *Creating is exhilarating*

By bringing awareness to your inner dialogue, you will cultivate a growth mindset which will give you the confidence to step into the unknown, embrace experimentation and imagine the infinity of possibilities for your art.

6. Cultivating Surprise

The Adjacent Possible is an experience of having one foot in the known and one foot in the unknown. It is a kind of relatable surprise.

This concept describes how each action taken by an agent in a dynamic and evolving environment changes not only the agent but also the surrounding environment.

It creates alternative possibilities that did not exist before, both for individuals in a system and the system itself.

I believe the adjacent possible concept is a foundational pillar of creativity.

Creativity plays a central role in the emergence of novelty in evolution, so it is perhaps not surprising that lessons from evolutionary biology might find fertile ground in the understanding of human creativity.

This is exciting news for artists. But the adjacent possible matters little unless you are aware of its existence.

The creative impulse can be subtle and easily missed or dismissed.

How The Adjacent Possible Manifests in Human Lives

Remember a time when you had an experience in your life where something astonishing or transformational happened that you did not know was possible beforehand.

It is when you get a hunch, when you hear a whispering in your ear, and this hunch or nudge may come from an entirely unique experience, such as observing nature or playing the cello or talking with friends or reading a book. You never know when it will show up.

Something new appears in your life and it initiates a sequence of events. It is up to you to allow this new experience to enter your life and art.

The adjacent possible is the idea that your act of searching in your art not only allows you to find the next step, it creates it.

A particular move, brushstroke or exploration opens up the adjacent possible, which is a new set of possible actions brought about by the original move.

This experience invites you to continue exploring and

stepping into the unknown in your art and life, experimenting as you go, and searching and moving deeper into the adjacent possible.

You are searching for something to emerge in your creation, and you are not sure what it is.

The State of Searching

The search and the state of searching opens the next possibility.

It is only by searching and making that move, that decision, that brush stroke that creates the alternative possibility which would not have been there if you had not searched and taken that step into the unknown.

This is about searching, acting, and responding to what you just did and seeing where it goes. It is continually evolving your work and not repeating yourself in your art.

And finally, the adjacent possible is about making room for surprise. This is about being *surprisable*.

A Story of Engineering Luckiness

Can luck be engineered?

Not in the conventional sense, like a bridge or a bicycle, but there are things that can be done to make one more "lucky." We first brought this up in Chapter Four, and now we dive deeper.

About 20 years ago, Dr. Richard Wiseman of the University of Hertfordshire in the United Kingdom decided to investigate the differences between people who considered themselves lucky and those who did not.

They found several hundred people for their study, half of whom considered themselves lucky and the other half unlucky.

They ran a controlled experiment of having them all buy cheap lottery tickets, looking for bias. Not surprisingly, winning lottery tickets did not correlate with perceived luckiness.

Further investigation in this decade-long study discovered two key features of luckiness that were ultimately published in his book *The Luck Factor*.

The first was that the "lucky" people had **numerous acquaintances** in addition to close friends.

Structured Surprise, Luck & The Adjacent Possible

The second idea is that of a kind of **structured surprise**. Lucky people did not over-schedule their lives, but left gaps that could be serendipitously filled.

They would engage in such behaviors as taking a different path to a store or to work, just because.

This was about leaving space for the unknown unknown. Something unspecified might happen.

This structured surprise is another word for the Adjacent Possible.

It is not so remote a reality as to be completely unrecognizable, but its adjacency means that it has one foot in your current reality and thereby allows you to take in something new and relate it to the familiar. You're still going to work, just taking a different route.

Lucky Lessons

How can these lessons be applied to the world of creativity? We touched on this question in Chapter Four. Let's explore it further.

The first lucky lesson, that of acquaintances, translates into having a passing familiarity with other creatives in your field, whether they be opera composers, painters, photographers, or screenwriters.

Not knowing them so well as to consciously emulate them, but well enough to take in what they have to offer and to walk through the doors they have opened ahead of you.

This is the realm of lineage.

The second lucky lesson translates into being open minded, observant and doing experiments. This is about making space for something new to fall in - and you don't know ahead of time what it will be.

Let Something Fall In

There's a German phrase *lass 'was einfallen* which translates literally to *let something fall in*.

It is a state of allowing- allowing something new to fall in that you could not predict otherwise.

The actual idiomatic translation is "You/I will think of something," but literal translations often expose philosophical underpinnings and origins.

Missing The Moment

We easily miss and dismiss our creative impulses.

These surprise moments can slip by unnoticed, so you must cultivate openness and awareness to capture them. Every mark you make on your canvas, every sentence you write, every move in your choreography creates the next possibility.

The evolutionary concept of the adjacent possible is analogous to what happens to you on your artist's journey. You are a microcosm of what is happening in the greater living world. How you create is derived from how the world creates.

Another way to think about this, or to imagine it, is that:

The act of moving forward creates a new set of next steps that would not have been possible otherwise. They would have been difficult or practically impossible to predict beforehand.

It is like a sequence of treasure maps, where each map guides you to a place where a new map hides. Now imagine that your act of searching not only allows you to find the next map, it *creates* it.

It is the next step, the adjacent possible to your emerging work and it is vital to you as an artist and creator.

The Adjacent Possible is about saying YES to creativity. It is about saying yes to the artist's journey and yes to your dreams of creating a meaningful art and life.

It is about crossing the threshold and saying yes to stepping into the unknown.

Creativity Accesses the Unknown

To evolve your art - whatever your art is - whether it is writing, painting, sculpting, choreography, composing music, filmmaking - you must be willing to *not know* ahead of time what is going to emerge.

It is about staying aware of the tugging in your heart, the whispers in your ear to create something new, to explore something that calls you, to experiment.

The adjacent possible is about the willingness to step out of the way and allow the mysterious to unfold.

Surprise yourself by what emerges. Allow for the *ugly art*, the messy manuscript, the flubbed line and realize that these "mistakes" are valuable.

Confronting and exploring the Unknown brings us to the following concept:

The sine qua non of being an artist is experimentation and continually evolving your art.

Embracing The Unknown

Every move you make on your canvas creates the next possibility.

The evolutionary concept of the adjacent possible is analogous to embracing the unknown.

Just as in reading a book, what keeps you reading is not knowing what is coming next and wanting to find out how it turns out. You are metaphorically laying the new track in front of you while seated on the train.

The destination is perpetually "TBD: To be determined," or perhaps IBD, "Is being Determined."

Searching & Finding Your Way in Your Art

One way to think about being an artist is that you are exploring and experimenting continuously. You are stepping into the place of *not knowing*, into the *terra incognita*, the unknown territory.

You are searching and you do not know ahead of time what is going to happen in your painting.

If I already know what's going to happen, it's all over.
—Michael Cutlip

This is not about following a recipe for your art. It is not about laying a Cartesian grid over your work.

Recall the story in Chapter One, when the artist, disgusted with her repetitive paintings, finally thought *What do I have to lose?* and plunged into wild experimentation. She simply did not know what would happen. She accessed the adjacent possible, had a breakthrough and surprised herself in her art.

7. Phase Transitions & Creativity

In science, phase transitions are the physical processes of transition between the basic states of matter: solid, liquid, and gas. Phase transitions occur in a dizzying variety of contexts from the physical to the social to the philosophical because they are about relationships between things, not the things themselves.

One well-known example is water becoming ice, a phenomenon that occurs suddenly at a very specific temperature.

Water, a liquid, suddenly crystallizes into a solid, ice. As the water cools, the ordering effect of crystallization prevails over the disordering effect of thermal motion where warm molecules move around more.

Crystallization

Once crystallization starts, it tends to spread, going from a minority of the water atoms to an overwhelming majority, one at a time, falling into place like dominoes, each fall enabling the next.

Water and ice are familiar to all of us, but the phenomenon of a phase transition is at its root more abstract and not specific to a material.

Imagine a network made of a collection of points and lines connecting pairs of points. This is very abstract, not contingent on any material or situation, and hence very universal. As more and more lines are randomly added to the system, the system begins to knit together, and it does so in a strange and remarkable way.

This phase transition, discovered by the mathematicians Erdös and Rényi in 1960, looks like this:

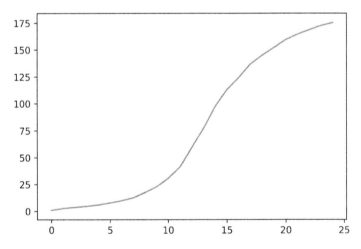

Phase Transition Graph

The steep part of the curve is the phase transition. The collection of points and lines goes from mostly disconnected to mostly connected, seemingly suddenly.

What causes this phenomenon of phase transitions? Dependencies upon dependencies. Cascades of connections. Accumulations of influences. Positive feedback.

Phase Transitions & The Paradox of Epiphany

Creativity and the relationship between creative practice and creative result is akin to a phase transition leading to epiphany.

The quietly invisible groundwork laid down by a disciplined creativity practice explodes forth one day as its disparate elements knit together, like a seed germinating and pushing forth into the sunlight.

Suddenly, *it all makes sense.*

But creative practice only appears to explode forth. The paradox of this epiphany is that underneath this phenomenon has been a quiet and gradual marshaling of energies, a knitting together of knowledge, context, and awareness.

You cannot jump straight to the epiphany; you must travel through the *not much going on* part of the creative process first. This is the nature of the creative life. It cannot be circumvented.

The 10,000 Hours

The 10,000 hours is a concept originally described by Anders Ericsson in his 1993 research paper *The Role of Deliberate Practice in the Acquisition of Expert Performance*.

Malcolm Gladwell, in his book *Outliers*, discusses the elements that fuel exceptional human achievement. It is a combination of innate talent, luck, and practice. He often mentions Ericsson's 10,000 hours rule.

Whatever talent and luck you have, there also seems to be a high correlation of spectacular success with spending hours upon hours at something to master it.

Miles Of Canvas

For artists, the 10,000 hours concept translates to miles and miles of canvas. It turns out that professional artists tend to paint a lot.

These 10,000 hours are like the flat part of the phase transition curve.

At first there is not much to show for all the hours you put into your work. The rewards are delayed but show up in an accelerated fashion later. It may not be fair, but it seems to be how things work.

To take your art, your creations, your skills further, you must hold on through the early phases of development when you feel awkward and do not see much reward.

It is grueling. It can feel disheartening.

You face the dark night of the soul of self-doubt over and over, wondering why you ever said yes to this endeavor in the first place. This is the moment of greatest despair.

But it is also the moment pregnant with the possibility of transformation — the transformation of trusting yourself even through the dark night.

The dark night will recur, even once you have mastered a subject. Nevertheless, if you hang on and move through self-doubt, trusting yourself in your daily practice, you will reap the inherent rewards of confidence, joy and moments of ease and creative flow.

You will be able to face the moments of self-doubt knowing that you can move past this phase. The grueling hours of facing disappointment, awkwardness and uncertainty will be worth it. The proverbial ice will melt.

8. Zero to One: You Can Start Anywhere

The Concept of Zero to One

Zero to One is an exciting mathematical concept that says that zero to one is the largest interval mathematically.

The difference between zero and one mathematically is larger than the difference between 1 to 2, 2 to 3, 3 to 4 and so on.

This can be understood through the idea of *mapping*.

A one-to-one mapping is a process where every member of one set is matched up with a member of another set.

An example is to imagine matching up every apple in a basket of six apples with six oranges in another basket.

Our mapping of interest is to take every number n from 0 and 1 and dividing it into 1, like so: $1/n$, the numbers from 0 to 1 are mapped onto the numbers from 1 to infinity. If your chosen number is $n = 1/2$, it maps onto $1/n = 2$.

If your n gets closer and closer to zero, $1/n$ becomes infinite. We know that $1/0$ is infinity. It almost seems like magic to take an interval from 0 to 1 and map it onto an infinite interval, but it is legitimate. Infinity is a strange and wonderful beast.

Bigger than the interval between 1 to 2 indeed!

And this interval between zero and one, from "nothing" (represented by zero) to something (represented by one), has enormous implications for artists.

The movement from nothing to something, from zero to one, is larger than the movement from something to something (one to two, two to three and so forth).

As artists we often find ourselves at zero when we are starting a painting, yet zero represents infinite possibility.

We are trying to move from zero to one, and if you think about the enormity of the interval in that movement, you see that it has tremendous implications for artists and creators.

Once we get moving, we are in a different class, so to speak, than those initial starting conditions, and so everything depends upon starting, upon going into your studio to paint, upon sitting down and beginning to write your novel.

Improving or modifying *something* is a lot easier than working on *nothing*, even if that *something* is not your best work.

You Can Start Anywhere

Just start, because that is the biggest movement, and the possibilities are infinite within zero to one.

As artists, we often procrastinate. We become fearful. We say to ourselves, *I don't know what I'm doing, I don't know what's going to happen,* which is a fantastic thing because as artists we do not want to already know what is going to happen in our art.

As creators, we are stepping into the unknown. The challenge is to realize the importance of beginning.

And once we begin, we have an infinity of options between zero and one. It is the most miraculous thing to simply begin.

Zero to One: Just Start

One of the things I find helpful when I feel resistance or procrastination to creating is to tell myself: *Zero to one, just start.*

Just begin. This is the biggest movement. Show up in your studio and begin. Begin your painting, your sculpture, your writing, your choreography, your film, your musical composition.

It is a significant thing to show up even when you do not feel like it. This is about going from procrastination and getting off the sofa to showing up in your studio.

It is especially important to start when you feel you do not have anything to express. That is oftentimes the excuse for not creating. And yet this is where we need to go- into the place of *not knowing*. This is where innovation happens.

There is an enormous chasm between doing nothing and doing something.

This is Zero to One. So, the question is, will you show up consistently to create your art? Will you say yes to Zero to One?

A Story About Zero to One

We know from mathematics that a vastness is contained in the space between zero and one. That unassuming interval contains everything.

Likewise, in life, moving from zero to one is everything. It is going from nothing, represented by zero, to something represented by one.

This is enormous, and it is something to take note of in your life.

I love this quote by Wayne Gretzky, the great hockey player, who said:

You miss all the shots you don't take.

—Wayne Gretsky

Not trying is an automatic no. Everything depends upon saying yes to starting.

Each Small Step Matters

You can "plea bargain" with yourself to begin something and that can sometimes work. Just tell yourself, *ten minutes in the studio and I can quit if I'm not into it*, or *I'll write four bars, and if it sounds awful, I can stop for today*.

A surprisingly large portion of the time you will keep going.

You can utilize the Japanese concept of *kaizen*, which says that each small step is important.

It is based on the philosophical belief that all things can be improved by continuous, almost imperceptible changes over time. like the accumulating phase transition in the last chapter.

Small changes make a big difference over time.

Story

There is a story of a wonderful writer who confided that when he finds himself resistant to sitting at the computer and starting his writing, he reminds himself of this concept of Zero to One.

He employs Zero to One by having a goal of writing 1200 words in two hours every day. He tells himself to write for and not worry about what happens on the page. 1200 words in 2 hours is one word every six seconds. Perfectionism needs to go out the window to keep that up, and that's OK.

He writes whether he feels he has anything to say.

Sometimes he does not hit 1200 words, but most days he does. It is the initial resistance of the surface tension of starting that he must break through.

Only rarely does he stop after he begins.

The act of starting invites you to continue.

It is a powerful practice to say to yourself something akin to, *Let's just start, zero to one. Let's put our toe in the water.*

For example, if you are going for a swim, you might not feel like swimming that particular cold day, but you can tell yourself, *I'm going to the pool. I'll put my toe in the water. After that, I can turn around and go home if I want.*

Often, you get in the water and keep going.

Imagine bringing this concept of Zero to One into your practice of creating. Get in there and start something.

Do anything, just begin.

Reflection On Zero to One

Reflect on the times when you feel resistance to starting, to going from Zero to One.

You read about the scenario of going to the swimming pool and putting your toe in the water, but it might be something else for you. It could be playing the cello or reaching out to a friend you have not talked to for a long while. You may be feeling resistance. There is a kind of getting over the hump of activation energy, like using a match to light a fire.

Notice what you say to yourself and how you feel when you procrastinate or avoid an experience.

I encourage you to get a blank journal and write about this and notice what shows up for you in your writing. If you do not have a physical journal, create a file on your computer to collect your musings.

Zero to One Exercise

Draw a line down the center of your journal page. On the left-hand side, write two or three big or small ideas that are calling you. These are ideas that may terrify you.

Something is calling you, but you are not quite getting there.

On the right-hand side, write down the smallest *kaizen* action to move you from Zero to One for each idea.

Ask yourself: *What is the first step I can take, even the smallest step, to begin to go from Zero to One on this idea that is calling me?*

It might be:

- starting a painting

- applying for an art exhibition

- writing a play

- auditioning for a dance

- transcribing on the cello and then moving towards composition

It can be anything. Whatever it is, document it in your journal.

It is not too big or small and it is important to you.

Write one, two or three things that are calling you and then write the first step that will break through the surface tension that is stopping you. This will move you into *Zero to One* action.

9. Experimentation & The Surprise Benefits of Ugly Art

The Importance of Experimentation

Creating is about experimentation, which is ultimately about accessing the adjacent possible and evolving your art.

In evolutionary biology, experimentation is usually called "variation"—life forms do not reproduce themselves exactly in most cases, so they are continuously experimenting as they reproduce. But they reproduce themselves closely. A platypus does not become a robin in one generation. But modern birds are descended from dinosaurs after millions of generations of experimentation.

Repeated experiments, provided you learn from them, can take you to amazing places.

The next generation platypus is very similar — *adjacent* to the previous one. Change too many things at once and the offspring are less likely to survive.

As artists, it is about the willingness to step into the unknown, to risk the ugly painting or the first draft or the flubbed line - to essentially say yes to continually evolving as an artist and creator.

This is a big thing.

Activate an attitude of experimentation in your work, and you will see amazing changes happening in your art.

The danger that lurks continuously is the tendency to say no and refuse the call of your dreams. You must step into the unknown, experiment and take big risks and allow whatever is trying to emerge in your art.

When you refuse the call of stepping into the unknown of deep experimentation, you stay in the safe zone of emulating not only others' artwork, but also your own.

Experimentation: The Handmaiden of Creativity

I had an 'aha' moment recently after talking with artists in our *Artist's Journey* and *Studio Journey* courses. We discussed the notion of painting for yourself, finding what you love, searching as you create, finding your way and continually exploring and experimenting in your art.

I observed each artist stretching and risking and wanting to take their work to the next level.

And I wondered, *if I had to give artists advice about the most important thing to access to accelerate your growth as an artist- what would it be?*

My first thought is that trusting and believing in yourself as an artist is crucial.

I also believe in the importance of working on *miles of canvas*, of creating as often as possible, ideally every day, or at least developing a consistent creative practice - 10,000 hours and all that.

Finally, to create your own unique art, to move beyond emulating the work of artists you admire, you must experiment. This is the willingness to step into the *terra incognita* — the unknown territory. This is where discoveries happen, where the surprises are and where new work emerges.

Trust, Experimentation & The Surprise Benefits of Ugly Art

Experimentation is intimately related to trust. We come full circle back to the importance of the inner journey. You must trust yourself enough to take risks, to not know what is going to happen and to allow for the unfamiliar, even the so-called *ugly paintings* to emerge.

Ugly paintings are vital for your evolution as an artist. They are the nascent, embryonic forms of new work emerging, new art trying to be born.

Creating Consistently

Creating consistently makes an enormous difference for your art.

The masters painted a lot.

The Museum of Modern Art in New York estimates that Picasso created over 20,000 works of art. That is one creation per day including weekends for almost 55 years. That probably does not include the works he painted over or threw away.

As you create many painting *starts*, you begin to see that no painting is precious. This gives you tremendous permission and freedom to explore and experiment in your art.

What we are talking about is the mindset of allowing yourself to step into the unknown, to search and find your way as you create, and to deeply explore and experiment.

It is in the state of experimentation that you will **search** (and this word is important!) and **find your way** as you paint.

We can feel you **searching** and accessing a state of **not knowing** inherent to the search and this is exciting, alive and mysterious.

It is **unpredictable**.

Experimentation sets the stage for surprise and your deepest art.

Searching & Finding Your Way in Your Painting

One way to think about being an artist is that you are exploring and experimenting continuously. You are stepping into the place of **not knowing**, into the *terra incognita - the unknown territory.*

You are searching and finding your way as you create.

You do not know ahead of time what is going to happen in your painting. This is not about following a recipe for your art. It is not about laying a Cartesian grid over your work and following a fixed procedure.

This approach is the antithesis of formulaic, predictable art.

Embracing Uncertainty

Experimentation is about embracing uncertainty

It is a wondrous thing when you trust yourself enough to experiment, to explore, to search and to not know what is going to emerge in your art. This is where the magic happens.

Astonishing art will not bend to your will.

You cannot force a painting to wow you.

But here is a secret: If you continuously explore and experiment and learn to tolerate expressions that are awkward, unfamiliar, even ugly — you will begin to create works that surprise you. You will create art that brings you closer to your deepest self-expression.

The possibilities for the emergence of astonishing art increase exponentially.

Story: Experimentation: "Let's Paint Some 'Ugly' Paintings"

Years ago when I was painting landscapes and figurative abstractions. My friend Sharon would call and say: *Hey Nancy, let's paint some ugly paintings!*

Sharon's exhortation never failed to evoke uproarious laughter. I was simultaneously exhilarated and liberated. She was the most experimental artist I have known and a writer as well. Sharon gave herself permission to create *ugly art* and it was a powerful lesson for me.

What if you allow yourself to paint whatever is coming through you at any given moment?

It is freeing to **let your creations live,** even the ones you deem ugly, and allow them to just be - to not go in and fix them but rather to sit with them for a while. These experiences are important. I believe this is a big part of trusting yourself.

Reflection

Think about the concept of failure.

Remember when you learned to walk? You fell repeatedly, but this did not stop you. Perhaps it made you more determined to walk.

When you learned to speak, you started babbling and then articulated one word. Soon, you strung words together and eventually achieved syntactical language. Think back on our discussion of phase transitions, with words being points and grammar taking the place of lines linking them.

Speaking and walking required trial and error. The same is true with art.

What is your biggest fear around failure?

If you let go and allowed yourself to play, explore and experiment like a child, what would you create?

Write about it. Write quickly, without editing or overthinking. Write anything and everything that comes to mind. It does not have to make logical sense.

Exercise: The Surprise Benefits of Ugly Art

This is about experimentation. It is about allowing the nascent embryonic forms to emerge in your art. These awkward forms may inform later works you create.

Keep track of your progress. Don't toss first drafts, you may find inspiration and reflection there later. Work in an art journal. Experiment with spontaneous painting and stream of consciousness mark making. Create freestanding vignettes, stanzas, melodies.

Do not worry about how your painting looks or your music sounds. Indeed, allow yourself to create the ugliest art you can imagine.

This is about expanding your ability to tolerate *ugly* art.

You might decide to work with a color you do not like, or you could create a messy painting using large pieces of charcoal. Maybe a very short concerto for twelve tubas. Whatever you choose, allow ugly works to emerge.

Keep these ugly paintings. Hold onto them. You will see if they show up in later works. Perhaps they will inform a new series of artwork.

10. The Paradoxical Freedom of Constraint

Simplicity is the ultimate sophistication.
—Leonardo da Vinci (1452 – 1519)

One of the most important foundational concepts for artists and innovators is constraint.

There is a power and potency in constraint regarding creativity.

There is a Latin phrase *multum non multa* which means much, not many. In employing much, not many, you go deep rather than wide. You explore a few things thoroughly, rather than many things superficially.

I love to think of painting, creating, and writing as employing simplicity and constraint and thereby going deep.

Constraint Is Paradoxically Limitless

The concept of constraint is so rich and diverse we could spend a lifetime studying it.

Even science is about constraint and abstraction. Science removes the extraneous and boils it down to the essence of truth. Doing so does not disrespect the complexity and richness of the natural world. Quite the contrary. It is a way of more deeply appreciating it.

An example: Isaac Newton (1643 – 1727) saw the pockmarked moon and the blue-green Earth of forests and oceans as two masses in motion around a common point, connected by gravity. Clouds and craters and myriad life forms did not matter in that context. All that richness was reduced to two points connected by a force. But that did not diminish the richness.

What do we mean by the word constraint?

The Oxford English dictionary defines it as a limitation or restriction. Synonyms for constraint include words such as restraint, control, curtailment, continence, discipline, discretion, reserve, self-command, even suppression.

Some of these synonyms may sound negative. You may ask yourself: *Is constraint really such a good idea as an artist?*

The Paradoxical Nature of Creativity

It sounds paradoxical that a key component of creativity and innovation is constraint.

This does not exactly fit the image of the free-spirited Bohemian artist or writer, yet one of the many paradoxes of creativity is the concept that within a constraint, within a limitation, is enormous freedom. This makes for exciting art.

Why is this the case?

The Elegant Solution

Scientists talk about the elegant solution to complex problems. The variables we deal with in painting, writing a poem or composing music are legion. Elegance and simplicity can be hard to find in that dense forest.

Here are some questions:

- How do you simplify things?

- What is the advantage of doing this in the first place?

- Why would you do this?

- How do you take a concept and boil it down to its essence?

- Why is this important?

There has been a great deal of research in creativity and innovation regarding the value of constraint and opening creative channels.

Improvisational Theatre

If you have ever explored improvisational theatre, you know they use constraints in the form of prompts.

You go on stage and discover a basket filled with folded papers that contain prompts. You randomly choose one. Written on the paper is a word or sentence.

This is the prompt for your improvisation. For example, it might say *you find a sparkly red handbag in the old woman's Cadillac.*

Your spontaneous responses to the prompt emerge for the next 20 to 30 minutes. You do not know where you are going in your enactment of the prompt from one moment to the next.

Each word and gesture unfold which opens the next possibility, a possibility that was not only invisible before but did not exist until you created it. It is a possibility contingent upon the steps taken before it. This is the adjacent possible.

Knock-Knock Jokes

A quotidian example of constraint is the example of someone asking you to tell a joke, but instead of saying, *tell me a joke*, they say, *tell me a knock, knock joke*.

Inherent in their request is the constraint of knock-knock.

This constraint helps you generate a joke. If someone asked you to tell a joke, you might draw a blank trying to come up with something. It is like trying to compose a joke out of thin air.

A knock-knock joke tethers the request, making it easier to improvise on the spot.

Specificity and tethering help unleash creativity.

The Hand

The human hand is one of the most powerful instruments of constraint.

It is a potent example of the paradox of the infinite freedom found in constraint. The shape and form of our hands has limited variations of usually five fingers on each hand with certain relationships to one another.

There is a limited range of motion of the fingers, the wrist and the opposable thumb, yet infinite possibility in this wondrous instrument.

From the moment of birth, we are searching, finding our way, and unfolding in this life. From the beginning, we have innate reflexes in our hands, such as the grasping reflex. If you place your finger in the palm of a baby's hand, she will grasp it immediately. This is a reflex, and it is surprisingly strong.

The hand is one of our most sensitive tools. Our hands and mouth are early sensors that help us discover our world through sensory-motor learning.

I am sure you have witnessed a baby exploring the world with her mouth. She places everything in her mouth because this gives her a great deal of information. There are robust neural connections in the mouth, and babies learn about the world through these connections.

Touch

We understand the world through our senses, and this includes more than seeing.

One of the most important senses is touch. Our hand becomes one of our most potent tools for sensing and understanding the world.

As a sculptor, I remember discovering the intelligence that lived in my hands as I sculpted a head in clay. My hands knew and felt the tilts, angles, and form of the head in ways beyond what I could see.

There is a *knowing* in your hands. It is a kinesthetic memory, and you can access this memory when you paint, write, and play an instrument.

Your hand reveals your individuality, your personal marks, and gestures. It has distinct movements, sensitivity, weight, pressure, firmness, looseness, quickness, slowness, lightness, heaviness, lyricism. It is particular to you, your personality, your history, and your aesthetic.

The actions of your hand reveal your own personal marks, signature, and lexicon as well as the deep intelligence in your body.

Structure In Constraint

Years ago, after seeing psychotherapy clients at my office I walked across the street to Stanford University to take an oil painting class. I came upon a group of jazz musicians who were attending the Stanford Summer Jazz Program.

We struck up a conversation and they invited me to a masterclass given that evening. It is burned in my memory.

It was a riveting lecture and performance by Steve Coleman, a young jazz saxophonist from New York.

He began by improvising on his saxophone, then stopped and talked about construction and deconstruction of the piece. He invited audience members to come on stage and improvise rap pieces on the spot.

It was pure magic.

I learned there is an underlying structure in even a seemingly unstructured piece. As the music seemed to fall apart, deconstructing, and developing into near chaos and disintegration, there was still a thread, a barely perceptible structure holding the work together.

Gradually the musician built the piece back up, increasing cohesiveness as if he had resurrected it.

The music became a living, pulsing, unfolding experience- and it was unpredictable. I think often of that talk given by the jazz saxophonist, and it still informs my work.

Even a bit of structure can be the nidus, the seed that can act as a catalyst for your work.

The structure may or may not dictate the expression of the piece or the form, but it may act as a constraint or counterpoint to bounce ideas off or respond to.

Bringing Structure into Your Art

Structure is an important concept in your art. You can map out a territory of a few constraints and allow your imagination to explore the reaches of those self-chosen limits.

You do not need many constraints, maybe one or two, because you already live with inherent constraints or structures. Your biology and physiology contain exquisite structures, such as the armature of your body, your skeleton, the wiring of your nervous system, the brain's protective casing of the cranium and the neural networks.

These limits yield unpredictable results, and this is what we want in our art.

Constraint: A Story

A student wrote: *My biggest challenge is choosing an idea from the many that keep me awake at night. My next exhibition is about boundaries, and I have so many ideas for it I don't know where to start!*

Does this story sound familiar?

A Million Ideas

You have a million ideas. You do not know where to begin. This is a good problem to have if you allow yourself to make decisions.

Creativity fuels possibilities and, paradoxically, constraint and decisions. The Latin word *decidire* means to cut through. You need to cut through the problems and infinite possibilities and be decisive.

My Story: The Potency of a Limited Palette

In the beginning of my painting journey, I could not wait to get into my studio and use bright, vibrant colors. I used mostly chromatic hues, lots of paint, and very little grayed colors.

My audience knew me as a colorist in my *plein air* oil landscapes and mixed media figurative abstractions. I reveled in jumping from color to color and surprising myself with novel color combinations.

I remember my teacher recommending using a limited palette, but I did not like the idea and resisted for years.

One day everything changed.

I saw the work of a dear friend and loved her use of neutral colors and scratchy mark- making. I admired her minimalist aesthetic and combinations of bronze, yellow, aureolin, parchment, and various green golds and yellow greens.

Inspired by the neutral palette, I began using constraint and exploring a limited palette of grays and neutrals with a bit of chromatic color.

Instead of using every bright color in my studio, I simplified my palette. I learned about the power of simplicity and constraint.

Constraint: Reflection

Surpassing all stupendous inventions, what sublimity of mind was his who dreamed of finding means to communicate his deepest thoughts to any other person, though distant by mighty intervals of place and time!

Of talking with those who are in India; of speaking to those who are not yet born and will not be born for a thousand or ten thousand years; and with what facility by the different arrangements of twenty characters upon a page!

—Galileo Galilei (1564 – 1642)

What will you communicate across time, across the centuries, through your art?

Using the constraint such as 26 letters or a limited palette, you can tap into an infinity of possibilities of self-expression.

Creativity connects to uniqueness, and uniqueness connects to decision. It is all connected.

If you do not decide, if you do not have constraint — you have chaos or repetition. It is neither gratifying nor interesting.

Explorations For Your Journal

Notice examples of simplicity and constraint in your daily life. Note these in your journal. You can also create a digital file of your observations and photographs.

It is important to hone your aesthetic vision. As you become more aware of the concepts of simplicity and constraint, you will see examples everywhere.

Sources might be from:

- nature

- science

- magazines

- haiku

- book covers

- fashion design

- Zen gardens

- typography

- minimalist musical compositions

- architecture

- music

- poetry

- literature

- imagery from dreams

Imagine using the concepts of simplicity and constraint as you create.

What will emerge? Write whatever pops into your mind without censoring. Notice what bubbles up for you and make a note of it.

The Six Maquette™ Exercise

When you are ready, get out a piece of paper approximately the size of a full sheet of watercolor paper. I have a fun exercise for you.

I developed The Six Maquette™ Exercise, informed by the great English sculptor Henry Moore, who loved to create hundreds of clay *maquettes* or little studies for his monumental sculptures.

Take your sheet of paper and mark off six areas of squares, blocks, or rectangles. You can use a China marker, a pencil, a graffiti marker, or acrylic paint.

You can work with a charcoal block, oil pastel, chalk pastel, graffiti markers, a big brush, thin brush, whatever you wish.

Do not overthink this. This is about experimentation and trusting your gestural expression, not perfection.

Choose your tool and make six moves, marks, or shapes on each of these six areas.

Do it immediately. Do not think. Do not plan. Do not try hard. Do not second guess. Do not edit. You can use your non-dominant hand, or switch hands as you go to loosen up.

When you have completed the six blocks, step back and look at your marks. These marks come from your energy and gestural expression.

You have a unique visual language. It is your lexicon and will thread through all your work. It's the genes of your artistic creature that lives within you.

11. Creative Evolution & The Adjacent Possible

The Artist's Journey: Creativity & The Unknown

The Artist's Journey is about creativity and the unknown and at its deepest level, it is about saying yes to your creativity, the adjacent possible and your dreams of creating a meaningful art and life.

A surprisingly large role is played by "mistakes" and "Ugly Art." It's not all unicorns and rainbows.

You are about to say yes to crossing the threshold and to stepping into the unknown in your creativity.

Creativity connects in fundamental ways to the unknown. It expresses itself in the ineffable, the inarticulable and the mysterious.

To grow your art and life, you must be willing to *not know* ahead of time what is going to emerge.

The Value of Mistakes & Ugly Art

Allow surprises to emerge in your art — the ugly art, the awkward silence on stage, the missed note on the piano and realize that these so-called mistakes are not only valuable but vital.

Here is an example of the power of mistakes: Since there are no sound recordings of Ancient Greek being spoken, it was challenging to figure out how people pronounced what they wrote.

Scholars got help in deciphering pronunciation from *spelling mistakes* made by scribes. They are clues that two differently written words or syllables sound alike.

It would have been much harder to piece together an unheard language without these mistakes.

The idea of a "mistake" is often a value judgment based on previous perception. You have created something that does not fit with your prior aesthetic point of view. It is easy to call it "Ugly Art," dispose of it, and move on. But ugliness has its place. It can be a signal for us to stop and pay attention.

What am I supposed to pay attention to? Something new may be trying to emerge in your art and at first you deem it as ugly. It doesn't fit in and bend to your will. It's not the art you were trying to create. It is unfamiliar and threatening. You don't identify with it and therefore reject it.

Ugly art is often the nascent embryonic form of new work emerging, new art trying to be born.

An astonishing series of paintings, an entire body of work may emerge out of these embryonic forms.

The Adjacent Possible: The Concept

The Adjacent Possible is a foundational concept for creativity we've been exploring in this book, particularly in Chapters Four and Six. It is a scientific concept from evolutionary biology that describes how each action you take in a dynamic and evolving environment changes not only your perspective but also the environment you are in because these two things are deeply interdependent.

It creates alternative possibilities that did not exist before.

The adjacent possible is the essence of creativity. It is part of the science that describes creativity.

Remember a time when you had an experience in your life where something astonishing or transformational happened that you did not know was possible beforehand.

It is when you get a hunch, a nudge, and this inkling may come from an entirely unique experience, such as observing children playing or walking on the beach or reading a poem. You never know when it is going to show up.

Something new appears in your life and it starts a sequence of events, and it is up to you to say yes to this and allow this new experience or these new things to enter your life and your art.

Your act of creating affects existence itself.

We are searching for something, and we are not sure what it is. This state of inquiry opens the next possibility.

It is only by searching and making that move, that decision, that brush stroke- that creates the alternative possibility which would not have been there if you had not searched and taken that step into the unknown.

It is searching, acting, responding, and seeing where it goes.

The Adjacent Possible is about continually developing your work and not repeating yourself in your art.

The Adjacent Possible: A Story

Have you ever opened the door to something new, not realizing it would lead to paths unimaginable?

A young woman studied piano, cello, and voice as a child.

Like many youngsters, she enjoyed piano and cello lessons, but balked at practicing during the week.

Voice lessons, on the other hand, were immune to her resistance. She had requested them from an early age and there was no issue with practicing.

Soon, it became clear it was time to stop piano and cello, as the child was adamant, she no longer wanted to take lessons and indeed, was no longer practicing the repertoire.

A few years later, when the girl was twelve, she attended a private school for grades six through twelve. This school was akin to a music conservatory, though it was a college preparatory school.

A Bluebird

A chance encounter with an older student at the girl's school changed everything. The music department held an annual cafe concert in which students explored repertoire related to jazz, contemporary or improvisational music.

At the cafe concert, a senior girl at the high school played bass in the jazz concert. The sixth grader admired the older girl's confidence and facility in playing the powerful instrument, perhaps especially because few women play this large instrument, let alone carry it around with aplomb.

The senior girl noticed the young sixth grader's admiration and responded with a thumbs up. That evening, the sixth grader told her mother: *I want to play cello again* and this was the beginning of the girl's musical journey. The young girl and her parents never imagined the decision to re-start cello lessons would lead to something heretofore unimaginable.

Cello lessons spurred an interest in Celtic music. Soon, there were annual summer Celtic music camps and summer solstice celebrations. The young girl played cello while flutists, guitarists and violinists played *Chanter's Tune* and a teacher recited Robert Burns' *Tam O' Shanter* in his hypnotic, rhythmic Scottish brogue transporting everyone to a place of legends.

Musicians played lively toe-tapping music, some from the repertoire of traditional Celtic music and other pieces that were original compositions. This experience inspired the young girl to explore lesser-known traditional Scandinavian folk songs and transcribe them for cello. Eventually, this led to composing original folk songs for cello.

The girl never imagined composing music for cello when she said yes to studying the instrument.

The Adjacent Possible Reflections

I invite you to notice moments when you say yes to something that leads to something unpredictable.

The adjacent possible is sitting beside you, waiting. It awaits your next step, your next move.

Do you notice it? Do you see it in your environment? It may be a small, quiet voice whispering in your ear, calling you to explore something new.

It may be the image that suddenly appears in your painting, or the character who emerges unbidden in your writings.

Write or make notes in your journal about your experiences with the adjacent possible. What comes to mind? When have you had these experiences? Are there certain situations or conditions that elicit them?

The Adjacent Possible Exercise

Cultivate the practice of the adjacent possible. This is about opening creative channels.

And there are various ways you can do that. You can:

- Say yes to stepping into the unknown

- Face your fears and go ahead, anyway

- Explore *maquettes* or little studies in your art

- Activate an attitude of experimentation, allowing ugly works to emerge and understanding their value

- Access different creative channels through music, dance, and sculpture

- Explore the relationship between the spontaneous and the considered in your art

- Say yes to the adjacent possible

These are some ideas to get you going on accessing the adjacent possible.

In painting or drawing the adjacent possible looks like making a mark and responding to it. One mark or shape creates the possibility for the next one.

In writing, set a timer for 20 minutes and write without editing, allowing your spontaneous thoughts to emerge.

In dance, it is the concept that one move informs the next.

In musical composition, it is noticing where the next note wants to go, and only by striking the first note or imagining the first note does the next note emerge in relationship to the first.

This is what we are talking about with the adjacent possible. Consider that this is about allowing and seeing the value in one action leading to the next.

It is also about strengthening your experimentation muscle, being aware of the adjacent possible and noticing when it shows up in your art and life.

Imagine I played a note on the piano, and that led to a fresh note or sequence of notes, which led to further notes or sequences of notes.

It is all connected.

Another example - imagine starting a painting, and an animal emerges. Then, you notice a story associated with the animal, and embellish the animal further in response.

One action leads to the next thing.

Take out a sheet of paper or a journal and begin writing about anything that comes to mind where you have accessed the adjacent possible.

12. Three Tips for Artists

Three Tips From 20 Years of Creating

An artist asked me to give her advice on how to develop as an artist. I thought about this carefully and realized there are three actions that make a big difference over time when practiced consistently. These are the three tips I shared with her:

1. Keep A Journal

Keep a journal to catalog your ideas. This is a powerful practice. This can be a regular journal — it does not have to be an art journal, but I encourage you to start one now. Do not wait. Get in there and play and experiment in your journal.

Whether you are drawing, writing ideas, writing stories, writing words- observe and document your aha's and revelations in your journal.

You can:

- Record ideas and questions that come up

- Document your inspirations

- Add non-text content like color swatches and color combinations that excite you

- Catalog your art- keep images or sketches of your paintings and notes about your creative process

- Explore the intersection of the arts and nature and your observations of texture and rhythms

- Play with ideas

- Note connections between art, psychology, science, mathematics, and creativity

You could play with little studies, *maquettes*, in your journal. The late British sculptor, Henry Moore, created thousands of clay *maquettes* to explore possibilities for his monumental sculptures.

Be wide ranging in your sources such as:

- your daily life

- theatre

- nature

- readings

- novels

- poetry

- dreams

- plays

- films

- daydreams

- and anything else that excites you

Your creations are also a journal of sorts. Pablo Picasso said his paintings were his diary.

Keep track of your art, perhaps:

- take pictures of them

    - date them

    - catalog them

    - add notes about what went into each work

- document the materials you used

- perhaps even what you were feeling at the time

2. Zero to One: Just Start

The second tip is to remember the concept of Zero to One from Chapter Eight and just start. By exploring miles of canvas, you accelerate your growth as an artist. You develop facility and confidence when you develop a practice of daily painting.

As we discovered in Chapter Nine, the pros paint a lot.

A Story

When I was painting oil landscapes, my teacher taught me it would be better to create many small panels, little four-inch by six-inch panels, rather than a few large works, because this would give me more opportunity to explore various possibilities for compositions.

That was a big teaching moment, and you might consider it for yourself.

Create lots of painting *starts* in your art journal.

3. Working in A Series

Related to the second tip of creating painting *starts* and miles of canvas, try working in a series and experimenting as you go. Do not worry about one painting or one piece of writing.

Nothing is precious. It is all experimentation.

When you activate an attitude of experimentation, you open creative channels, and you are on fire with creativity.

Working in a series nudges you to explore the adjacent possible.

The adjacent possible is the idea that your act of searching in your art, in your writing, in your choreography not only allows you to find the next step, it creates it.

It would not have been there otherwise if you had not taken that move. A particular move or brushstroke or exploration opens the possibility of the next one, the adjacent possible which occurs by action.

And so, with that, let us step into the unknown.

13. Three Massive Mistakes Even the Pros Make

The Old Way

The old way of creating art is not working. It is rule bound, formulaic and predictable.

It says, if you just have more techniques, you will be great. It is riddled with self-doubt, inner criticism, second guessing, perfectionism, and the tyranny of technique.

You struggle with starting, with ideas, emulating others, with repeating yourself, getting stuck in the middle, frozen, fearing ugly art and finishing.

The new way, a new approach to solving this predicament, is a game changing mindset shift that will transform your art and your experience of creating it.

The Big Idea

I call it the Big Idea. It is something I have been thinking about and implementing for years.

I asked myself, *if you could distill down to the few things that make it or break it for you in your art, and your life for that matter, what are those things? What is that process? What is the elegant solution?*

And I realized that it has to do with one overarching concept. What we are talking about is the Inner Journey. The big idea is that the Inner Journey affects everything — your mindset, your psychology, your belief and trust in yourself, or lack thereof. It affects your art, your creativity, and your life.

Art is an inside job.

It has far-reaching implications and potential consequences. It is the holy grail, and it affects three vital studio practices at the core of creating as an artist.

By learning these three practices, you will overcome inhibitions, activate your creativity, never run out of ideas, fall in love with painting and create paintings that wow you.

And it is based on science, psychology, and research in creativity.

I asked myself, *what are the few things you need to do consistently as an artist to transform your art?*

I found that there are three massive mistakes artists are making, even professional artists, that are standing in the way of creating art that is astonishing and alive.

Story

Before we get into those, I will tell you a personal story. For as long as I can remember, I have wanted to live my most creative and meaningful life, to say yes to my dreams. And at times it has been a struggle. Perhaps you can relate to this.

When I was 17, I was grappling with existential angst. I was bored with school.

I stayed home a great deal my senior year and read *The Inferno*, the first book of *The Divine Comedy* by Dante Alighieri. Immersing myself in the story, I felt I was not alone. Dante was there beside me, speaking across seven centuries of finding himself in the dark wood, lost.

Like Dante, I was at a precipice - about to leave for college and feeling both excited and unsure. Dante was stepping into the unknown and I was too.

Fast forward a few years and something called me. It was medicine.

The day I finished seven years of medical training, something else called me, the siren song of art in the form of sculpture. Pretty soon, one thing unfolded into the next and I was drawing figures, painting watercolors, oil still life and landscapes and working with collage and mixed media. I knew I wanted to move in the direction of abstract expressionism.

I loved Cy Twombly, Joan Mitchell, Helen Frankenthaler and I wanted to paint like them. I tried to replicate the work I loved, but this was a dead end. The paintings didn't satisfy me.

I got busy in my medical practice and my art floundered. I was not expressing the paintings I imagined, and I felt like giving up, but something in me just could not let it go.

There comes a day when you face yourself and your darkest, deepest doubts- when you wrestle down the dark angels of angst and despair.

The deeper truth I discovered was I wanted to paint like me. I wanted to explore the reaches of my own imagination.

One of the lessons I learned over the years in being an artist as well as working with artists in workshops and classes is that **being an artist is ultimately an inner journey.**

While you learn concepts, principles, and techniques, you find out these are guides, but they are not the thing itself. To get to your deepest work, it is about stepping into the unknown. It is about adopting an attitude of *not knowing and* cultivating exploration and experimentation in your art.

It is about moving closer and closer to your own self-expression.

Technique is valuable, but it is only there as a tool to support expression. You do not lead with technique. This is a big shift artists come to sometimes after years of focusing on rules, constructs, and techniques.

This is a whole new journey. You step into the unknown and face yourself in the dark night of the soul of your deepest self-doubt. On the edge of that dark night is the transformation of trusting yourself.

Expressing Your Own Art

We have been looking at the problem of creating your most meaningful art in the wrong way. It is not really a problem, but rather an opportunity.

If you want to open creative channels, move past resistance and feel freed up and liberated in your art, trusting your own voice and vision- here are the principles, strategies, mindsets, and concepts that will help you get there.

I am going to show you the foundational concepts and practices from the intersection of creativity, science, evolutionary biology, mathematics, and psychology of creating your most surprising, astonishing experimental work as an artist.

The Big Idea is that it is first and foremost about your Inner Journey. Creating art is fundamentally psychological.

Whether you are at the beginning of your journey or a seasoned professional with your work in galleries and museums, the big secret I learned is that:

Your inner landscape, your inner dialogue, your mindset is your most important asset because it affects everything.

Your inner landscape affects your ability to:

- face your fears and self-doubt, and go ahead anyway

- start creating

- move through the messy middle

- decide when to finish your painting

- take risks, play, explore, and experiment in your art

- keep going when you get frustrated

- tolerate and embrace ugly art

Your Inner Journey is about trusting yourself. It is about developing a growth mindset - the sense that your possibilities for growth and improvement are limitless. It is about noticing your inner narrative, learning ways to speak to yourself that promote curiosity, inquiry, and a positive approach to challenges.

This is about noticing fears and self-doubt that arise and addressing them in a mindful way, asking yourself, *what if I trusted myself in this moment, with this painting?*

By imagining the possibility of trusting yourself, facing your fears and wrestling down the dark angels of self-doubt, you strengthen your ability to believe in yourself.

3 Massive Mistakes Even the Pros Make

Let's turn now to three massive mistakes artists make that cause them to not love their art. In fact, they may be feeling disillusioned with their art.

We will start with mistake number three and build up to mistake number one.

Massive Mistake #3: Painting Paralysis

This is a condition where an artist is so afraid of making mistakes, she fails to start. The fear of doing something wrong overtakes her desire to create.

To start is quite literally to begin. It is to cause something to come into being.

The problem is you simply do not start, or you do not paint enough. You are not painting miles of canvas.

It takes everything to start one painting - and then you get hung up on that one painting, making it precious. You take that one painting and work it to death.

You may work on one painting for months, and then are devastated when you do not love it, when it flops, when it is muddy and has lost the feeling of aliveness you created in the beginning.

Soon, you avoid your art altogether because it is so painful.

Story

Years ago, I painted *plein air* landscapes. Once a week, I met with a group of artists and set up my easel. I painted one to three paintings in a three to four hour stretch.

If I had a great session, I noticed the next week I felt anxious about whether I could replicate last week's success. The pressure mounted and I dreaded facing the easel. How would the painting turn out? I would be devastated if the painting flopped.

This tension sucked the pleasure out of painting and sometimes I avoided painting altogether.

I simply was not painting enough and therefore could not gain traction. What I did not know then that I know now is that the pros paint a lot.

So, what is the solution to this mistake?

Start

The solution is to start. So, let's start with start. We discussed the Zero to One concept from mathematics in Chapter Eight. To go from nothing to something is an enormous thing.

Imagine that you have been avoiding your studio. It has been a few days. The last time you were there, you created a painting you thought was terrible.

Not wanting to repeat the experience, you find other activities to distract you. The longer you wait, the harder it is to show up.

This is where Zero to One comes in. If you can say to yourself,

- *Let's go in there and mix some paint, Zero to One.*

- *Maybe I'll explore mixing orange and green to get variations on citrine, Zero to One.*

If you can remind yourself that it is about starting, starting anything, this will help you get back into your art.

It is not about creating a masterpiece. It is about starting, and you can start anywhere.

It is a freeing. liberating and miraculous thing to simply begin.

Lots Of Starts

One of the ways you can play with Zero to One in painting is by creating many *starts*. We call it *lots of starts*. Pretty soon you are creating a series of *starts*.

Why is this important? By beginning, by creating *lots of starts*, you:

- open creative channels that lay dormant

- access unfettered self-expression

- move past creative blocks that hold you back and cause you to avoid your art

- reduce the probability of getting overly attached to a particular artwork

By creating *lots of starts*, you create:

- a sense of permission

- a feeling of allowing

- an experience of opening exploratory mark-making

- an opportunity to loosen up your art

- an attitude of playfulness and exploration

All of this helps move you past avoidance and procrastination. If you do not start or allow for *lots of starts*, the danger is you will begin to avoid your art, or you will be increasingly frustrated because your art is not progressing.

Worst of all, you may decide to give up entirely on your art.

Tip

Here is a tip for you in your studio. Go into your studio. Take out sheets of paper and create 3 to 10 stream of consciousness mark-making *starts*. Do not censor, judge, or edit.

Allow for exploratory mark-making. You may decide to create these while listening to music.

When you are done, choose 1 or 2 *starts* you would like to work up further and do that. Keep the rest of your *starts* raw and let them live *as is*.

This is a great exercise for accessing your gestural expression, your particular and unique lexicon of mark making.

Let's now move on to mistake number two.

Massive Mistake #2: Licking the Paint

Licking the paint is when you are not confident enough to make decisive moves in your art. Instead, you make timid adjustments hoping to create a masterpiece.

This issue manifests itself in many contexts, from endless editing of manuscripts to obsessing over performance instructions for a piece of music.

I see this mistake often. It manifests not only in licking the paint, but also in a reliance upon technique to create successful paintings.

The Tyranny of Technique

This is where artists look outside of themselves for answers. They look for a step-by-step, how-to formula for their paintings. They emulate others and look for validation of their art through critique and praise.

Technique is a false idol.

The danger is painting by committee, art that is boring and soulless. It is the lowest common denominator art.

These artists believe they will become a great artist once they learn all the techniques.

Another variation on this is the belief that if they buy all the tools and supplies, they will get better at art. They go from workshop to workshop, technique to technique, searching for the Holy Grail for years.

They think art is technique. But one day they realize that art is not technique.

Art is not technique. No amount of technique will move you closer to expressing your deepest art.

They take technique classes, and their paintings look like everyone else's- repetitive and formulaic. They could take a hundred technique courses and still not create the paintings of their dreams.

Technique is painting from the outside in,
rather than the inside out.

Instead of focusing on the big ideas, the foundational concepts and principles that are akin to the root and the trunk of the tree metaphorically, they focus on technique.

Making technique primary is like focusing on painting the leaves and details. They think it will knit together and lead to a great painting, but it does not work like that.

It is about coming from the deeper foundational concepts that inform your creations and allow you to express your own true art.

Here is a story.

Story

For years, I pursued technique. I thought if I learned the right technique, I would finally make paintings that wowed me and my viewers, but it was an elusive thing.

Before I knew it, my paintings looked strategic and contrived, as if I was following a cookbook formula. Eventually I got bored. The paintings, while technically good, simply did not move me emotionally.

One day I had a breakthrough. I was tired of repetitive paintings. I was disillusioned with looking outside myself for the answers.

One night, an image of continuous line snaking across a canvas came to me in a dream. The next morning, I decided to create exploratory studies of minimal line and marks.

26-piece assemblage

I created a 26-piece assemblage of studies and was at first uncomfortable. They did not look finished, yet I realized they had an immediacy and aliveness I had previously never attained.

I allowed them to just be, to live *as is*. This was an enormous breakthrough for me.

I also realized the power of working in a series rather than making one painting precious. Most importantly, I realized the power of experimentation.

Experimentation

Let's talk about the power of experimentation.

The mark of being an artist is being one who experiments continuously, not resting on your laurels, not satisfied with the status quo.

It is about stepping into the unknown, embracing mistakes and the unpredictable. It is about tolerating *ugly paintings*, because there are surprise benefits of ugly art as we discussed in Chapter Eleven.

What If?

A powerful way to access experimentation is to ask yourself the question: *What if?*

Allow your mind to both wonder and wander. Ask yourself: *What if I try this? What if I try that?*

Whatever it is, allow it. It could be exploring a rectilinear Cartesian grid under-structure. It could be creating bulbous shapes. It could be employing a one-color palette. It could be anything that evokes excitement, meaning or aliveness for you.

Why is experimentation important?

Becoming a great artist is about the movement of coming closer and closer to who you are. It is about reaching the fullest expression of who you are in your art.

The answer is not technique. No amount of technique will get you there.

Technique is only there to facilitate expression, but it is not expression itself.

Do not lead with technique. What takes you there is the willingness to experiment, which is based on trusting yourself.

Here is what happens to artists who avoid experimentation —
their art stagnates. It becomes boring and predictable.
Worst of all, the artist begins to doubt herself and feel like
an imposter.

Tip

Write quickly, without thinking, one to five things that pop
into your mind that you want to experiment with in your art.

There is power in listening to the creative impulse.
Sometimes it is subtle. Make a note of anything you want
to try.

Start with the question: *What if?*

List one to five things that comes to mind.

The Number One Mistake

Now it is time for the number one mistake artists make, and
it begins with a story.

After years of painting figures, landscapes, and abstract
expressionist paintings, I understood the importance
of many *starts*, miles of canvas, working in a series, not
licking the paint, moving past emulating others, and deeply
experimenting.

Yet I still found myself creating art that did not wow me. I was not loving my art and I kept wondering why.

What is it that I am not understanding? What is the missing piece?

Finally, I had a conversation with my partner, Dr. Bruce Sawhill, Stanford educated theoretical physicist and mathematician who revealed a concept from science that changed my experience of creating art.

The Sawhill Secret

I think of it as The Sawhill Secret.

It is about how creating art is a process of continually evolving, not only starting, and experimenting, but continuing to evolve your art.

This is a game changer for creating astonishing art, art that wows you. And it relates intimately to mistake number one.

Massive Mistake #1: Empty Virtuosity

Empty Virtuosity is a success disaster.

This is when an artist mines a vein of high-grade ore until it is completely exhausted, after which she finds herself empty-handed and at the bottom of a deep hole.

In essence, she repeats herself in her art and in the process loses sight of possibility.

This is when the artist has moved past paralysis and past looking outside of herself and emulating others' work. Just when she thinks she has that solved and is on her way with deep experimentation- she hits mistake number one.

This is when the artist repeats not others, but herself.

The danger of winning, of creating successful astonishing art, is the danger of repeating yourself. We learned of this peril of the success disaster in the story of the artist in the first chapter.

The artist falls back on repeating, returning to what she thinks is the solution, the formula for what works.

Paradoxically, the artist no longer lives at the edge of the unknown. She is no longer creating astonishing art.

The Mining Metaphor

If one mines the vein to the last shovelful, one finds oneself at the bottom of a deep hole with nothing left. The artist takes her success and drives it into the ground through repetition. She takes it down to death.

The artist becomes so focused on success she loses curiosity, discovery, and expressiveness in the flash.

So, what is the solution? What is The Sawhill Secret?

The Adjacent Possible Framework

The Adjacent Possible Framework is about evolving your art. The essence of being an artist is continually evolving your art. One form unfolds into the next. It is like being in a river. It is ever changing and never ends.

What we are talking about is the *Big Momma* of all practices - the groundbreaking concept from theoretical evolutionary biology, the adjacent possible.

Let's apply the adjacent possible concept to creativity.

The Adjacent Possible is the idea that each step you take illuminates possible paths forward that were not only invisible before, but did not exist before because your action changes the environment you are in.

It is co-evolution; it is co-creation.

It is akin to the Heisenberg Uncertainty Principle in theoretical physics, where the act of observing changes what is being observed, while in The Adjacent Possible your act of creating affects existence itself.

It is mind blowing. Every move you make on your canvas is opening the next possibility, the adjacent possible, that would not exist if you had not made that move.

Do you see this is about continually evolving your art, continually unfolding into the adjacent possible, continually creating a new reality with your art?

I think this is one of the most exciting concepts. Imagine exploring this in your art.

Cultivating Surprise

What we are talking about is cultivating surprise.

You simply do not know what is going to happen next. And this makes for astonishing, unpredictable, unique art — art from you- your gestures, your experiences, your impulses.

So why is evolving your art, The Adjacent Possible Framework important?

Being an artist is about continually evolving your art, allowing it to unfold and not be reduced to formula or prescription. It is about reaching for your fullest self-expression and getting to the elusive deepest work you yearn to do.

It is about stepping into the unknown, into the adjacent possible and cultivating surprise. This is where the most astonishing art comes from.

It is the essence of creativity. Indeed, it is the science of creativity.

Start, Experiment & Evolve

Evolution has two parts: experimenting and selecting. Selecting relates to decision. Without either one of them, it does not work. There are no experiments without *starts*. So, it is all connected: start, experiment, evolve.

We begin with the inner journey because your psychology affects everything. Then we cultivate three key actions: start, experiment and evolve.

It is not about copying others or yourself — that is a dead end.

The danger of not employing The Adjacent Possible Framework is that you spend years trying to figure out why your art does not excite you.

Meanwhile, your art stagnates, and you feel bored. You have a lack of enthusiasm for your art. You lose confidence. You repeat what has worked before. You fall back on safe, predictable, formulaic art.

You simply do not reach your dreams of the elusive deepest art you yearn to create.

Here is a story of an artist who did not know how to access the adjacent possible framework in her art.

Story

An artist finally began to trust herself and cultivate experimentation, and she thought she was on her way. She told herself: *You've got this* - only to find the siren call of so-called success reeling her back in with its clinging tentacles, beckoning her to repeat her successes and to repeat what has worked before.

Like the artist in the first chapter, she sold out her solo exhibition. She was on a roll and found herself wanting to repeat her success. She told herself: *Hey, it was experimental. It was surprising and astonishing. Maybe I can do that again.*

The Nibulator

The *nibulator* nibbles at artists to carve out a body of work that sells, even though each piece is barely distinguishable from what the artist created before.

The reality is it is hard to paint in a whole new direction for every exhibition, but if an artist can continually evolve at the edge of that work and not simply repeat the work with slight variations *ad infinitum*, she will be on her way to creating astonishing art.

The Faustian Deal

The artist thinks: *I'm on a roll here. I'm winning.*

But unbeknownst to her, it is a Faustian deal. Pretty soon, the artist has developed a body of work that is relatively indistinguishable from the last work she created.

She is circling. She is repeating, not someone else's art, but rather her own.

This woman was in tears, confiding she felt like a fraud, not a real artist. She knew her paintings, though successful, were predictable. When she viewed them, it felt as though they were mocking her. They were diluted facsimiles of what she was capable of. She was losing her love for her art. She felt like giving up.

Success Disasters

When artists hold onto their successes, like the artist in Chapter One, even though they have started to stretch into the unknown, into experimentation, it is a problem. This tendency to fall back on the known, the familiar, the winning formula is seductive, but deadening.

Another danger is spending tens of thousands of dollars looking for answers in tools and techniques, trying to learn how to make art you love.

Lastly, perhaps worst of all, the danger is you reach a point of such deep frustration you throw your hands up in resignation, giving up on creating the art of your dreams.

You must learn to evolve your art. Specifically, you must learn the science of creativity, The Adjacent Possible Framework.

If you do not, you may take your art to the experimentation stage, but you will miss out on the most important part - evolving your art, taking it from the unknown into the unknown unknown, to the stratosphere of wow, to that place of continuing evolution.

Many artists run around, working hard on their art, trying tools, trying techniques, trying to create art that stands out. They waste thousands of dollars and hundreds of hours of precious time on tools, techniques, and strategies that do not work.

They want the excitement of creating art they love. They want to express themselves and share their art with the world and feel proud of it - but without mastering evolving their art, specifically, The Adjacent Possible Framework, they will feel like Sisyphus, forever rolling the ball up the mountain but never finding what they are looking for.

You Are an Artist

You are here to express your deepest, most meaningful art, art that is dynamic, alive, and evolving.

I see many artists struggle to create art they love, art that is unique to them. They get frustrated and feel like giving up as artists because they do not know how to go deeper and access the adjacent possible effectively.

They hit a plateau. The creative impulse is calling them, nudging them to take the next step, to step into the unknown, but they are scared.

They turn their face away, retreating to the safety of the known.

Even though they sometimes put their toe in the waters of experimentation, they are not evolving their art. And it is tragic because it does not have to be this way.

And so, we come full circle back to the inner journey - how your relationship with yourself, your psychology, affects your ability to face your fears, trust yourself, and keep going to the edge — to that place between creation and collapse.

This is where the juice is.

14. Four Traps Artists Face

Four Traps

Working with hundreds of artists every year, I see a recurring theme of artists saying *I feel like my art does not measure up to what I want it to be.*

How can you change that? Many artists transform their work, and the way they do this is by overcoming the four traps where artists get stuck. You may recognize yourself in this and see where you are getting blocked.

My artist's journey is that I identified as a doctor first and then realized I was also an artist and that being an artist is an *inside job*.

It is an inner journey. It cannot come from the outside.

As artists, we may think we are the only ones who experience this. Observing many artists over the years, I see recurring patterns on this artistic journey.

It is a path riddled with perils. As artists, we travel through these perils, and I see four big traps on the journey in moving closer and closer to the fullest expression of who you are in your art.

No one outside of you can properly critique this movement.

Trap #1: The Critique Trap

This story is about the belief that the answer is outside of yourself.

A Student's Story: The Pursuit of Critique

A student in my workshop approached me and asked,

Will you give me an art critique? Will you tell me what to do to make this a great painting? I'm not happy with it.

Another variation on this theme is:

Can you give me some idea of what is not working in this painting? I have been working on it for a while, and nothing I do seems to make me feel happy.

This story from my workshop is one I call the pursuit of critique.

The student looked outside of herself for answers for her art. If only someone would tell her what to do, what to create — she would be on the road to mastery.

The problem is that when you look outside yourself for how to create art, your art looks like someone else's solution.

Your art becomes formulaic and predictable. It becomes generic. Your paintings look like all the other students' paintings who are following the how-to steps laid out by the teacher.

The challenge is to paint like you, not the teacher, not peers, not the masters.

To paint like you requires intrinsic validation. This recalls the poem *The Wild Geese* by Mary Oliver.

It is a poem about self-compassion. Its opening lines say it best.

You do not have to be good.
You do not
have to walk
on your knees
for 100 miles
through the desert
repenting.
You only
have to let
the soft animal of your body
love what it loves.

—Mary Oliver

Trust yourself to love what you love and to express what you love. Let us see *you* in your art. The most exciting and alive paintings show us you.

You may wonder and think to yourself, *yes, but how do I create great art?*

Imagine being at your canvas and someone is giving you an answer for what to do with your painting. The problem is it leads you away from yourself, from trusting your own creative impulse and even from the subtle, inarticulable, embryonic ideas that bubble up in your imagination.

The creative impulse is often subtle. Blink and you'll miss it.

The only way to capture the creative impulse is to stay present and connected with yourself. The risk of outside influence is your art may become someone else's vision, biases, opinions, ideals, rules, and aesthetic. This is tricky territory.

The deeper risk is that your subtle, creative impulses get covered up and silenced with too much outside influence.

The tendency, when looking outside yourself for answers to your art, is your paintings become predictable, formulaic, and strategic.

My approach is to help students ask themselves a series of rhetorical questions so they can self-assess their own work. This is what I did with the student in this story.

Rhetorical Self-Assessment of Your Art

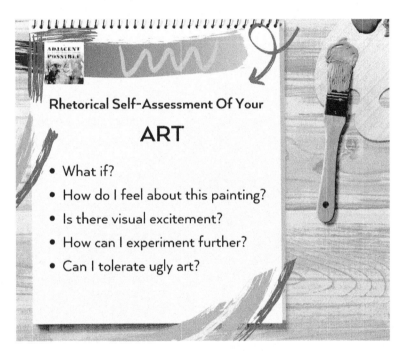

Rhetorical Self-Assessment Of Your ART

- What if?
- How do I feel about this painting?
- Is there visual excitement?
- How can I experiment further?
- Can I tolerate ugly art?

The first question I like to ask is: What if?

Ask yourself this question. *What if I try this? What if I try that?* Notice where your mind goes. Access the reaches of your imagination with this overarching question of *What if?*

This singular question activates and unleashes exploration and experimentation.

The second question is: How do I feel about this painting?

Ask yourself this question and see what you notice about this feeling. Stay tuned into your intuition about the painting. *How do I feel about it? Do I like it or not? Do I want to stay with this, change it, veil it or cover it up?*

Can I allow this painting to exist even though this is uncomfortable?

The third question is: Is there visual excitement?

From a biological perspective, the eye likes to be excited. It especially notices value contrast, edges, movement. There are many ways we can create this.

We can use the principles of art to create visual excitement and yet not be hamstrung by rules.

The fourth question is: How can I experiment further?

Can I take it further into a series?

Can I imagine allowing this painting to live as an experimental, exploratory work?

The fifth question is: Can I tolerate ugly art?

As you experiment in a series and evolve your art, mistakes and ugly art are bound to appear. The painting you view as awkward and ugly today may be the unfolding of surprising art that will knock your socks off tomorrow.

Do not be in a hurry to get rid of ugly art.

Don't Be Ruled by Rules

Sounds like a rule, doesn't it? Art is riddled with paradox.

We are talking about cultivating an attitude of exploration and experimentation, tuning into your intuition, working with principles and concepts, yet **not being ruled by rules.**

My Story

I am reminded of my story of grappling with this issue of looking outside of myself, looking for a teacher, an expert or other artists to guide me when I did not like my painting. I thought they could tell me what to do to fix my painting.

One day, at a master's residency, I created a painting with a large orange shape along the left side. A wonderful artist and good friend saw the painting.

She did not like the big orange shape and told me I could improve the painting if I got rid of this shape.

I followed her advice and knocked back the orange shape, but I still was not happy. In fact, I felt the painting was worse, and I liked it better before I messed with it.

It seemed as if I had ruined the painting.

I tried to recover the original freshness of the painting, to bring back the orange shape, but I could never redeem the painting and, after multiple attempts, ended up rolling it up and packing it away in my closet.

The lesson I learned is to trust my intuition about my art. This is the only way it will truly be mine.

Old Belief

The old belief you say to yourself is: *The answer is outside of myself.*

New Belief

The new belief is: *The answer is inside of me, and always has been.*

It is like Dorothy in *The Wizard of Oz*, who finally realized the answer was not with the Wizard, the man behind the curtain. It was inside of her the entire time.

The truth lives inside your body, in your gestural expression and the lexicon of your mark making. The challenge is allowing it to be expressed unfettered.

Your Style Will Find You

Do not worry about finding your style. Do not search for it. It will find you.

In the process of deep exploration, of experimentation, of doing the work, your style will emerge. It is your signature, your lexicon.

When you learned to write, you followed instructions on how to write. Soon, your signature emerged, a signature unlike anyone else's in the world. It is unlikely you worried about finding your style in your signature.

You have a unique signature, an exquisite lexicon that belongs to you. Your job is to get out of the way and allow it to emerge.

When you try too hard to create a style, it shows. Your art looks forced.

The hardest work is to trust that your voice, your vision, your lexicon, your marks, your gestural expression, and your style will be expressed.

I believe if you finally trust, if you finally let go- you will see something astonishing unfold. Your irrepressible spirit will show up and become visible.

Move beyond your strategic ego and allow the brilliance and uniqueness of your soul to shine through. Express that which only you can express.

Rather than a critique, look for a guide who will help you assess your own work by being able to ask yourself deeper rhetorical questions.

Trap #2: The Imposter Trap

The imposter trap is a story you tell yourself expressing self-about your right to be an artist.

It is the belief that says:

- *I don't have the credentials or body of work of an artist*

- *I didn't come in through the right door to call myself an artist*

- *I don't have the pedigree of an artist*

- *I don't have my own style*

- *I don't deserve to be called an artist*

- *I never went to art school*

- *I went to art school, but I still don't feel like an artist*

- *I don't have connections with gallerists and publicists in the art world*

- *I gave up being an artist years ago because I was told it wasn't a practical career*

- *I'm not a real artist*

I often hear artists say variations on these themes in my workshops.

Others say:

- *I'm not an artist because I can't express what's inside of me onto the canvas*

- *I'm not original*

- *I'm not that creative*

- *I don't know what to create, so I copy the work of artists I admire*

- *It's too late, I'll never catch up*

Story: The Pursuit of Identity

This is story is about the pursuit of identity. You feel you are not a genuine artist because you have learned innumerable techniques and followed a set of formulas. You follow the rules.

Yet you still do not love your art.

My story is that I had difficulty calling myself an artist, even though I had been painting for over 10 years. My identity was as a doctor, first and foremost.

How could I be both a doctor and artist? I went to medical school, not art school.

One day, my friend Sharon urged me to enter two of my paintings in an exhibition in Pacifica, California. I almost declined. I had never entered my art in a show, plus; the juror was a famous artist, Terry St. John, and

I knew the competition was stiff, especially from artists in San Francisco.

I could submit only two artworks for the show. I submitted two figurative watercolor paintings.

To my astonishment, both paintings were accepted into the show. At that moment I realized I had been holding myself back by believing I could not be both an artist and physician.

It had seemed like a stretch to be both because medicine and chemistry, which I had studied, were scientific and seemingly the furthest thing from art. Yet, I realized that I could bring together the disciplines of medicine and art.

Student Story

I have a wonderful story of a student who came into my workshop and confided she felt like a fraud. She had never attended art school and while she created amazing fiber art pieces, quilts, and textiles, she felt she was not a real abstract artist.

I could see the influence of her background in textiles in her intricate, layered mark making and textures.

One day she created a piece that moved me to tears. It had a childlike innocence and playfulness that reminded me of the words by Rilke.

Oh, hours of childhood

It is part of a longer poem. These words haunt me because they speak about the fleetingness of time, especially of childhood.

Here is an excerpt from the poem:

Oh, hours of childhood,
when behind each shape,
more than the past appeared
and what streamed out before us
was not the future.
We felt our bodies growing
and were at times impatient to be grown up,
half for the sake of those
with nothing left,
but their grown-upness.

—Rainer Maria Rilke

I shared this poem with her, and she cried. She had told herself her works appeared chaotic, disheveled, and almost psychotic. She devalued the rawness and immediacy of her work.

She explored a rhythmic painting exercise I teach in my workshops and classes. I love this exercise because it confers a tremendous sense of freedom. It allows and records your unique, gestural expression as it comes through your body onto the canvas.

She started working with this rhythmic exercise and loved it. She was on fire, and now, several years later, is a prolific abstract artist known for her rhythmic mark-making.

Old Belief

The old belief is *I am not a real artist.*

New Belief

The new belief is *I am an artist, and I am the one who decides this.*

An artist creates art, and the problem is we are not embracing this definition because we feel we do not have enough skills or techniques.

But the problem is a mindset issue. Only you can decide and

call yourself an artist.

Trap #3: The Judgment Trap

The judgment trap is a story about being terrified of facing and expressing yourself because you feel you do not know what you are doing.

You are afraid of judgment, both from others and yourself. At the deepest level, you feel vulnerable about putting your art out into the world because it brings up insecurities.

One person told me she was a people pleaser. She was afraid of standing firm in her own two feet and taking up space, of being seen, of owning her art without feeling the need to explain or apologize.

Some artists say they feel judgment because others have told them being an artist is indulgent, frivolous, decadent, and selfish.

Story: The Pursuit of Validation

Here is a story. One artist said, *I'm terrified of expressing myself in my art. What if it's not any good?*

I call this The Pursuit of Validation.

Years ago, I created abstract horse collages on full sheets of watercolor paper, and I had a following. But one day I felt the urge to develop the work further. I wanted to create large, abstract, mixed media paintings of horses. I was not sure how I was going to do this.

How would I translate the horse from collage to painting, from a small canvas to a much larger one? This question puzzled me. I wasn't sure how to begin.

Eight months elapsed and still no large abstract horse painting was to be found.

One day I asked myself, *what have you got to lose? You can always cover it up with gesso if you don't like it and start again.*

I grabbed some paints, a large brush, and a bucket of water. I loaded the brush with acrylic paint and made my first large gestural brushstroke.

That one brushstroke broke the surface tension and was the fundamental change that led me to where I am today as an abstract artist.

Zero to One

Just begin. This is a concept from mathematics we explored in Chapter Eight revealing that the biggest difference, the largest interval, between numbers, is between zero and one. It is like going from nothing to something.

Do something, anything. You can start anywhere. Just start.

If you dislike it, you can always cover it up and begin again. Who knows? You might love the brushstrokes you made.

Here is a story from a student I worked with.

Student Story

The student was staring at the canvas in front of her, frozen. She could not make a move.

She felt paralyzed by self-judgment, inner criticism, second guessing and the fear that she would make a wrong move and create a terrible painting.

She said this often comes up for her after a good painting session. Fear arises when she has created a painting she likes or even loves. She becomes afraid the subsequent paintings will not hold up to the painting she loved.

The next time she comes to the canvas, she is afraid she cannot maintain the winning streak and create like that again. She worries it was a one off, a fluke.

I guided her to see, by asking her a series of rhetorical questions, that it is not unusual for an artists' inner critic to show up after creating art you love. Creating is a vulnerable experience. It brings up fear - the fear of failure, of exposure, of rejection.

It is not unusual for inner criticism to rear its ugly head after creating a great painting. You fear you will never paint like that again.

I guided her to think of painting as the experience of creating exploratory studies and experimental works.

Old Belief

The old belief is *I am terrified of facing and expressing myself in my art because others may judge me, and worse, I may judge myself.*

New Belief

The new belief is *I came here to be myself, to express my deepest, most meaningful art and life. I experiment deeply and paint for myself. Bringing joy or meaning to others with my art is a bonus. The worst thing I can do is refuse the call of my yearning to create art.*

Say yes to the idea that you paint for yourself. You did not come here to please anyone, rather, you came here to be yourself — to express your deepest, most meaningful art and life.

Trap #4: The Technique Trap

A pervasive trap for artists is to focus on technique. We explored the tyranny of technique and its relationship to empty virtuosity in Chapter Thirteen and you can read about it and my story there.

Reprise: The Inner Journey

Have you noticed how all four traps have a commonality of going outside of yourself, of looking for the answers out there?

It is what keeps us trapped because the work of being an artist is ultimately an inner journey.

To summarize, what you need to believe, the inner work you need to do is:

- Know that your art is an inner journey of self-expression

- Believe that you have your own signature, lexicon, and style

- Decide that you are an artist - claim it

- Trust yourself, experiment, and paint for you

We do this work inside of ourselves. This is inner work. The problem of going outside of ourselves is what keeps us trapped.

Practical Next Steps: The Ugly Painting Practice

You may wonder, *how do I work with this?* There is a practice I call The Ugly Painting Practice.

It is a powerful concept for releasing the inner artist. It is a practice that has helped hundreds of artists create raw and expressive paintings.

This is a mindset shift of activating an attitude of allowing, because we understand that there are surprise benefits of ugly art. Innovation is fueled by mistakes, failures, and ugly art.

Being an artist is about continually evolving your work. It is not about repeating formulas that work. It is about going to that edge, stepping into the unknown and taking the leap. It is about experimentation.

To innovate and develop your work, you must be able to allow for and tolerate the unfamiliar, the unusual, the paintings you hate, the ugly paintings.

The secret is trusting yourself.

To get to your deepest self-expression in your art, you must explore the depths of yourself and the reaches of your imagination.

We get stuck because we look for the answers outside of ourselves. This is about looking inward. We dive deep and look inside ourselves as we explore the inner landscape that affects our art.

This is the process you need to move through to get to the elusive, deepest work you yearn to do.

This deepest work is the work of my life, both in art and psychiatry, guiding artists and creators to believe in themselves. These creative concepts will help you consistently and confidently create art that is authentically you.

Say Yes to Your Dreams

I invite you to imagine your big dreams. *What are your big dreams for your art and life?* I invite you to go deeper into your heart's yearnings, to express yourself in your paintings and to create your deepest art.

The risk here is not doing the work you are here to do.

As an artist you are on this journey, this life cycle of creation. You yearn for something — for a feeling of meaning and aliveness and it calls you forth into the journey, into something new, into the unknown.

15. Three Invisible Paradoxes

Your Dreams

You are here for a reason. You have dreams waiting to be expressed. You want to unleash your creativity and live your most meaningful life.

You may be working on an exciting dream. Maybe that dream is writing a book. It might be filming a documentary or singing opera, drawing animals, painting abstract expressionist works or choreographing a dance.

Maybe your dream is about planning and executing an expedition to the Antarctic or learning a new musical instrument. Perhaps you want to transcribe and compose music or learn photography or a foreign language.

Whatever your big dream or goal, it is exciting for you, and you want to do everything you can to achieve it.

You may be solving a problem, a big, painful problem in your life. Things might feel challenging for you. Maybe you are overwhelmed with a new creative project. Perhaps you have suffered a serious setback or disappointment.

Whatever your situation, it's important to believe in yourself and know that you can solve this problem.

Your heart has its reasons for your dreams, and you are here in your life, on this earth for a reason. You have come here to express yourself. You matter. Your stories, your art, and your dreams matter.

There is no one like you in the universe. You are irreplaceable and unrepeatable. You are a miracle.

You came here to be yourself, to live your deepest, most meaningful life. No one has the chemistry, biology, gestures, quirks, or history you have.

You were born with the power to create and make a difference in the world. This is inherent to you. It is not something outside of yourself, but the brilliance within you right now in this moment.

Even though I am a psychiatrist and have helped people with personal development and life issues for over two decades, I am not here to give answers. I am here to guide you to ask questions and reflect on your life to bring forth the treasures that live inside you.

The poet Rilke said:

Live the questions. Be patient toward all that is unsolved
in your heart and try to love the questions themselves,
like locked rooms and books that are written
in a very foreign tongue.
Do not seek the answers which cannot be given you
because you would not be able to live them, and
the point is to live everything.
Live the questions now.
Perhaps you will then gradually, without noticing it,
live along some distant day into the answer.

—Rainer Maria Rilke

Embracing Uncertainty

What we are talking about is embracing uncertainty. There are answers inside you waiting to be found.

As you step into the unknown, into the mystery of who you are, you will live the questions. You will experience aha's, revelations, understandings, and the unfolding of wisdom.

All of this begins with you saying yes to the dreams that call you.

But here is the thing,

If:

- any area of your life is a struggle

- things are not going well

- you reject your creations

- you see your art as ugly or mediocre

- you hate your first draft

- your choreography sequence seems off

- you flubbed your lines in the play

Guess what? Be excited. Yes, this is where you want to be.

The Paradox of Creation

Creating takes the known world and spins it on its head because creating is about embracing the unknown and ultimately understanding the value of mistakes and ugly art.

This is about crossing the threshold into *not knowing*, a vulnerable place to be.

Creating is not about replicating what you know.
This is about allowing the emergence of fresh forms,
new associations, the unseen and the invisible.

I remember my first sculpture lesson. I was a newly minted psychiatrist and my first dream, the day I finished seven years of post-medical school residency training, was to find a sculpture teacher and learn how to sculpt.

I was too intimidated to take a class, so I found a sculptor, Adrienne Duncan, who would teach private lessons.

When I arrived at Adrienne's house with 25 pounds of clay, I said, *I don't know what I'm doing.*

Adrienne said, "Great!"

At that moment, I knew I had found my teacher.

And with that, let's dive into the three invisible paradoxes of activating the creative life of your dreams. We are going to talk about how to move through three paradoxes of activating your creativity.

So here is what you will learn:

- The one thing you must do to create. It is a game changing concept from mathematics, but you do not have to be a mathematician to implement it.

- Stories you tell yourself that keep you from activating your creative life.

- The Holy Grail of creating and how this will transform your life and art.

Invisible Paradox #1: The Refusal

You tell yourself it is safer to stay in the known, in the familiar, in the status quo.

And you refuse the call. You turn your face away from the dream, the yearning, the whisper of something you want to explore.

The problem is, the dream will not go away. It keeps showing up, nudging you, whispering in your ear.

Your refusal causes pain.

What the Refusal Feels Like

You go to a bookstore to the self-help section and feel the familiar yearning to write your book on parenting teenagers with compassion. The problem is you have sat on this dream for years and feel disappointed that you put it off. It feels like an ever-receding aspiration that will never come true.

You experience the pain and disappointment of unlived dreams. It is the feeling that something vital is being missed.

You feel as if you are not living your most meaningful life, and it is a feeling of regret.

What the Refusal Sounds Like

This is what you may say to yourself:

- *It's too late*

- *I don't know what I'm doing*

- *I'm not that creative*

- *I'm not really an artist, dancer, opera singer, musician, actor, filmmaker, or writer*

- *I'll get to it later — I'm busy*

- *It's not realistic to do this*

Refusing The Refusal: Opening Possibilities

But when you finally say yes to your dream, when you finally refuse the refusal, you open the field of infinite possibilities, and this is because saying *yes* equals possibility.

So, what do you do? How do you say yes to the things that scare you so you can get closer to your dreams?

Zero to One

The solution? Zero to One.

What is Zero to One, and what does it have to do with creation? And how does it move you past Invisible Paradox Number One?

As we discussed in Chapter Eight, Zero to One is a mathematical concept. It is the idea that the interval between zero and one is larger than any other interval — it is larger than the interval between one to two, two to three and so on.

Zero to One means that the biggest change is from zero to one, from nothing to something, from no to yes.

Zero to One has enormous implications for creativity. When you make a move, any move, you are moving past inertia, past zero to action even when you tell yourself you do not know what you are doing.

Story

This is a story of a woman who turned her face away from her dream of creating art for 42 years. She wanted to paint, but she had three children, an ill husband, and a full-time job as a teacher.

Time slipped away.

One day she looked up, and she was 64. Her children were grown. Her husband had healed, but her dream had lain fallow.

Soon she felt the familiar tugging at her heart. She would scour social media looking at paintings by artists, the voice in her ear asking, *What about my art? Is it too late?*

At first she ignored it. She had not painted since college. She would be rusty, not remembering how to paint, or worse, she would be mediocre. The voice nudging her to paint; however, would not be silenced.

One day she drove to an art store. Hands trembling, she filled her basket with eight tubes of paint, five brushes and ten canvasses. *Who do I think I am?*

Despite self-doubt, she knew deep down she was on her way to creating art again. *It is important to hold on to your dreams no matter what.*

Truth

When you finally say yes to your dream. When you finally refuse the refusal, the universe steps in to help you.

When you are living your most alive and vibrant life, you are:

- taking risks

- experimenting

- exploring

- evolving in your life

What we are talking about is cultivating a life of meaning and living your most alive and vibrant life.

Fact: You have what it takes to say yes to your dreams, to bring them alive.

Let's turn insight into action: Write about your dream. Be specific. For example, maybe you want to write a screenplay within the next year. Whatever your dream is, document it.

Writing brings visibility to your dreams and confers value.

Recap

- Decide on your dream

- Say yes to your dream

- Bring your dream into action

- Zero to One

This is how you overcome Invisible Paradox Number One.

Invisible Paradox #2: The Perils

The perils are those real or imagined consequences of saying yes to your dream and plunging into the unknown, into the underbelly, into the bowels of the monster.

The problem is the perils can paralyze you and make you think you made a mistake in saying yes to your dreams.

You doubt yourself and your abilities. The old familiar life beckons you to turn back. These perils are about fear, because creating brings up fear. It brings up vulnerability.

What the Perils Feel Like

You finally say yes to your dream only to plunge into the perils of:

- fear

- self-doubt

- perfectionism

- inner criticism

- second guessing

- overthinking

- feeling lost

- resignation

What the Perils Sound Like

This is what you may say to yourself:

- *Oh, no, I don't have what it takes*

- *This is too hard*

- *I'm not good at this*

- *I should give up*

You have so much self-doubt you feel like going back to your old life, the one where you ignored your dream.

So, what is the solution?

When you finally say yes to your dream, when you refuse the refusal and move past the perils, you open the field of infinite possibilities.

Fear Is a Good Thing

It turns out that fear is a good sign, because fear means you are facing your edge.

My Story

I had a dream of speaking on stage at an author conference but was terrified. I wanted to speak about creativity to a group of 400 writers in Austin, Texas.

To do this required a three-minute online audition. I got to the finals only to learn I now had another hoop to jump through- a two-minute online audition.

A part of me felt like giving up. It was already hard enough to get my message across in a three- minute speech, how could I do it in two minutes? Even if chosen, I had plans to travel to Italy and would have little time to craft a 20-minute speech for the stage.

I almost gave up, but something inside, a little voice said, *don't give up. Your message is important, it could make a difference for someone.*

I did not give up. I spoke on stage, and many authors came to me afterward saying how much it meant to them to hear my talk.

But one woman stood out. After my speech, holding her hand to her heart, she confided she had lost her 17-year-old daughter to a massive pulmonary embolism six years previously. She said my talk gave her courage to continue writing her legacy book about her daughter so future generations in her family would know her daughter's story.

The inner voice had told me it might touch someone who needed to hear my message.

Your art can change someone's life. Remember this as you face the fears inherent to creating.

How do you keep going in the face of fear and perils, so you can get closer to your dreams? How do you move beyond fear? What does it have to do with creation, and how does this move you beyond Invisible Paradox Number Two?

The solution is to face your fears and go ahead anyway.

Truth: Fear exists for a good reason

Fear is an indicator you are stepping into the unknown, into unfamiliar territory and taking risks.

Fear developed to keep us alive. It harkens back to saber-toothed tigers, of dank caves and of lives, precarious and short, death sudden and vicious.

This history passed along the centuries through our DNA lurks inside of us in the older, more primitive structures of our brains- a sleeping giant ready to awaken at any moment.

But there can be too much of a good thing. Living a life based on fear can stop you from achieving the highest expression of your humanity, much less attaining your dreams.

Fear Can Be Mediated

Awareness can mediate fear. We begin to recognize the inner monster as a phantom rather than a real-life Grendel your inner Beowulf must slay.

It is important to keep going, even when you are afraid.

Fact: You have what it takes to face your fears and mediate them through awareness.

Exercise

Get a pen and paper and ask yourself, *what are my fears?*

Turn your insights into action. Write one to three of your biggest fears on the left-hand side of the paper.

For example, your fears might be:

- *I don't know what I'm doing as an artist*

- *I'm not really a writer*

- *I'm too old to be an actor*

Now, on the right-hand side of the paper, replace each fear with a positive statement.

For example,

- *It's a good thing to not know; creators are continually stepping into the unknown*

- *I am a writer*

- *Writers write, and that's what I do*

- *Now is the perfect time for me to act*

- *It's never too late*

Recap

Let's review:

- Face your fears as you plunge into the unknown — this is where the magic is

- Go ahead anyway

- Replace your fears with positive statements

Fear is a good thing, and what we are talking about is cognitive restructuring.

Cognitive Restructuring

Cognitive restructuring is the rewiring of neural networks through mindfulness, awareness, and reframing. What you say to yourself matters. You can rewire your neural networks.

This is how we overcome Invisible Paradox Number Two.

The paradox is that fear is good. It means you are at your edge; you are stepping into the unknown, and this is scary, but it is also meaningful.

Now let's move on to:

Invisible Paradox #3: The Dark Night of the Soul

You finally push through the refusal and say yes to your dream, and you face the perils of creation only to reckon with The Dark Night of the Soul when all feels lost.

The problem is that the dark night of the soul is the moment of greatest self-doubt and despair.

It is the moment you must face alone because you are ultimately facing yourself. No one can do this for you.

What the Dark Night of the Soul feels like:

- You are in the middle of a 300-page draft of your novel, and you lose faith in the project and in yourself

- You feel like ripping it up, abandoning it

- You feel convinced that you are not an actual artist or writer or choreographer, filmmaker, poet, composer

- All feels lost

What the Dark Night sounds like:

This is what you may say to yourself:

- *What was I thinking?*

- *How did I ever think I could do this?*

- *Why did I say yes to this?*

- *Who are you kidding?*

The paradox is that the dark night of the soul, the moment of greatest self-doubt, is the moment pregnant with possibility.

Transformation lives at the edge of your struggle.

This is the time to hold on. Facing the Dark Night equals transformation, and that is because facing the dark night, facing yourself, leads to the transformation of finally trusting herself.

So, what do you do?

Your solution is to dig deep and carry on through the dark night. Hold on through self- doubt, knowing that transformation is on the other side.

Do not give up on the manuscript, the play, the comedic routine, the choreography, the musical composition, the painting, the feature film, the poem.

What is the transformation? What does it have to do with creation, and how does it move you past Invisible Paradox Number Three?

The transformation is trusting yourself.

The transformation is wrestling down the dark angels of self-doubt and despair and trusting yourself.

Why is this important?

The essence of being a creator is experimentation and evolving your art, and this requires self-trust. You must trust yourself enough to take risks.

Artists create. They continually develop their work, explore new and unknown forms, and allow themselves to be surprised by what bubbles up from their explorations.

Sherry Carter-Scott said:

> *Ordinary people believe only in the possible. Extraordinary people visualize not what is possible or probable, but rather what is impossible. And by visualizing the impossible, they begin to see it as possible.*
>
> —Sherry Carter-Scott

A Story About Rembrandt

This story about creativity would not be complete without talking about Rembrandt.

When I was a child, I was fortunate to have two Rembrandt reproductions, *Man with a Golden Helmet* and *Girl with a Broom*, hanging in the living room, where I played.

Staring at these figures for hours, I imagined they were real and could at any moment step out of the canvas and play with me. Such was the power of great art.

When Rembrandt was 25, he painted the most innovative group portrait ever seen, *The Anatomy Lesson of Dr. Nicolaes Tulp*. No one had ever before placed figures in a variety of positions in the picture plane in a group portrait. His arrangement of figures was unique. This painting placed him in the history books, cementing his fame.

Rembrandt was one of the first artists to fully transform self-portraiture to a sophisticated genre. Not only that, but Rembrandt also experimented with pigment mixtures that are still not replicable.

He created textures by scratching into the paint with the handle of his brush and explored impasto brushstrokes. He took risks and moved into unknown territory, exploring the reaches of his imagination, and this is part of why he is considered one of the greatest artists the world has ever known. Rembrandt experimented and continually evolved his art.

The Adjacent Possible

This is our now familiar concept from evolutionary biology, and we have been discussing the dynamic where one thing not only affects the next but helps create it.

One movement, one opening, leads into and opens possibilities that would not have been there otherwise without taking that step.

Each step on your journey generates a new set of possibilities and each action you take in a dynamic, evolving environment changes not only your perspective but the environment you are in - it is akin to Heisenberg's Uncertainty Principle, but more complex than just making an electron hard to pin down.

It creates alternative possibilities that did not exist before, and I believe this is the essence of creativity.

It is what creating is about. It is that which is around the corner, just around the bend of this reality.

It lives in the unknown, waiting for us to discover it.

Exercise

Take out a piece of paper and write about an experience where you almost gave up but did not. Somehow you held onto your dream. You moved past the dark night of self-doubt and trusted yourself enough to keep going.

You took a step and something new emerged that would not have otherwise, and things that you had no way of knowing would happen beforehand happened.

This is the adjacent possible.

If anything pops into your mind about an experience where something led to a surprise, that there is no way you could have known ahead of time, you were stepping into the adjacent possible.

Recap

The paradox is that the dark night, the moment of greatest self-doubt, is the moment of transformation.

By facing your fears, you activate the possibility of trusting yourself. Your deepest work lives at the edge of your struggle, so hold on through the dark night.

We come full circle to activating the creative life of your dreams. Here is a brief review:

We talked about the three keys to the creative life of your dreams.

- Say yes to your dreams

- Refuse the refusal

- Believe and trust in yourself so you can explore and experiment deeply and evolve your art by accessing the adjacent possible

You are a creator, your story, your art, your creations matter. You are precious and irreplaceable. The world wants to see you in your creations and what you must share.

Beliefs are the authors of behavior.

Your thoughts inform your action and inaction. Studies in neuroscience show that you can transform your thoughts. You can change your neural networks and think in novel ways.

Your inner dialogue, which reflects your inner landscape, matters. How you speak to yourself has far-ranging implications for your life. Believing you can grow and evolve makes a big difference in opening possibilities in your life.

May you trust yourself, create many *starts*, cultivate experimentation, and evolve your art and life by accessing the adjacent possible.

16. The Adjacent Possible Creativity Challenge

We are what we repeatedly do. Excellence,
then, is not an act, but a habit.

—Aristotle

Miles Of Canvas

As an artist one of the most important concepts is to show up in your studio and do the work. The pros create a lot.

You are more likely to develop a robust studio practice like the pros if it is something you truly want. Your big Why, your reason or reasons for creating and being an artist, will help you move past resistance when things get tough by unleashing your resourcefulness, perseverance, and motivation.

The Power of Habit

An influential study by Phillippa Lally, PhD at University College London, found that it takes an average of 66 days to form a habit.

Lally's research also revealed that missing a day here and there does not hinder the habit-forming process. Lally says you are more likely to be successful by only forming habits you genuinely want to incorporate into your life.

The next step is to set up cues that will prompt you to complete them.

The idea is to lower the resistance to initial starting conditions, much like adding a drop of oil to remove surface tension.

For example, if you want to paint daily, have your paints, markers, water buckets, paper towels and paper, canvas, or panel ready to go in a prominent place in your studio or in a corner of a room. If you have little space, set up an art cart with paints, brushes, paper and markers.

If you want to work in your art journal daily, have your journal available along with pencils, markers, and paint in a prominent place in your studio so you'll never forget.

If you're a cellist, lower the resistance to practicing by having your cello case partially open and music on your music stand ready to be played.

Lally's work says the idea is to concentrate on:

1. remembering to do the habit

2. staying motivated

In creating a habit, you want to get to the place of automaticity, the experience of acting without thinking.

When researchers plotted the results of how long it took people to establish a habit, they found a curved relationship between habit and automaticity.

The earliest repetitions were the most beneficial in establishing a habit, while the gains gradually diminished over time.

The Adjacent Possible Creativity Challenge will set you on your way to establishing a robust daily studio practice. Getting to this place of automaticity, where you don't have to think about it, you just do it - is the consistent practice to help you become a prolific artist.

The Rewards

By committing to *The Adjacent Possible Creativity Challenge* you are building a foundation of success as an artist, for the rest of your life. By waking up each morning committed to your daily studio practice you develop **discipline, grit, and an exploratory and experimental attitude** that will take you to the stratosphere of *Wow* in your art.

In addition to developing successful habits of a daily, robust studio practice, you will strengthen the **growth mindset** you need to believe in yourself as an artist.

You will understand the importance of the Inner Journey, your psychology, as well as implementing three key actions: *Starting, Experimenting and Evolving* in your art.

Lastly, with one foot in the known and one foot in the unknown, you will access **the adjacent possible** in your art and life.

Steps To Begin

Step 1: Register for The Adjacent Possible Creativity Challenge

Visit www.artistsjourney.com/TAPBook to register for *The Adjacent Possible Creativity Challenge* video workshop.

Step 2: Plan Your First Day of The Adjacent Possible Challenge

Commit to your first *Adjacent Possible Challenge* and schedule it in your calendar. Remember, the concept of Zero to One. Just start.

Step 3: Get Support

Go here to www.artistsjourney.com/TAPBook and join *The Artist's Journey Community and become one of "TheAdjacents"* in our wonderful community of wildly experimental artists. You'll find encouragement and inspiration as you develop your daily practice of saying YES to your art.

Epilogue

The price of doing what you believe in is, and always was,
the same — namely, your life.
—Heinz Pagels

Creating your deepest art and life is a Herculean task but worthy of the effort.

It begins with saying *yes* to your dreams.

It takes everything to listen to your heart's yearnings, answer the call, and plunge into *the mystery of creating* with aliveness, meaning and your own true voice.

As T.S. Eliot speaks of '*the unknown, unremembered gate*' in his poem *Little Gidding,* I am reminded of the ineffable experience of life unfolding and how we come full circle back to ourselves.

We shall not cease from exploration
And the end of all our exploring
Will be **to arrive where we started**

And know the place for the first time.
Through the unknown, unremembered gate

In the last stanza, Eliot reflects on the notion that it requires everything to live your deepest life.

Not known, because not looked for
But heard, half-heard, in the stillness
Between two waves of the sea.
Quick now, here, now, always —
A condition of complete simplicity
(Costing not less than everything)

—T.S. Eliot, *Little Gidding*, the last of the four quartets

Creating from your source, from the place of *not knowing*, rather than emulating other artists' work or your own is the central concern of this book.

Your Inner Journey Affects Everything

Your mindset, your psychology, your belief, and trust in yourself affects your art, your creativity, and your life.

The End Is the Beginning

It requires conscious effort and awareness to stay curious and hungry as an artist. Mental exercises and grit are required to keep one foot in the instability of the adjacent possible and the other planted in your current reality- a kind of existential yoga.

Like yoga, it is a practice and is not innate.

In fact, it goes against nature's programming that tells you to stop exploring and start exploiting once you've found something good.

You could play it safe- but a part of you wants to step forward and take risks and so this book is an invitation to evolve your art and life.

Being an artist is about continually evolving your art. Being a conscious human is about continually evolving your life.

Herbert Simon received the Turing Award in computer science. He had a thesis he milked for all its variations, and it led to paths he might never have imagined.

In the Disney movie *Mwana*, the girl sails away from her island and her culture on a ship that was concealed for years. Her people were nomadic but had settled on an island and kept the ships in good repair, hidden under a waterfall.

Mwana found the ship and was able to journey to new places.

May you keep your ships in good condition.

Quieting The Inner Critic

As artists, it is important to make mistakes, take big risks and quiet the inner critic. There are surprise benefits of allowing and embracing mistakes, mishaps, and ugly paintings. This is where creativity lives.

The German word for mistake is *fehler*. But *fehlen* means to be missing, to be absent, so the idea that a mistake is an absence of something is inherent in the word - but perhaps it is the presence of something, too.

Maybe mistakes are an essential part of the process of creating. It should not be viewed as purely an absence of something nor as necessarily a bad thing.

You need failure. You embrace mistakes as a key part of the learning process. Who knows? You might just fall in love with your mistakes.

Full Circle

The adjacent possible can be the guiding principle for your creative life, a beneficial framework for your artistic endeavors.

You are a creator. You are irreplaceable. Your voice, your story, your vision, your expression matters. You make a difference in this world, and we want to see you express yourself in your art.

The great late poet Mary Oliver asked in her poem *The Summer Day*,

> **Doesn't everything die at last and too soon? Tell me, what is it you plan to do with your one wild and precious life?**
>
> —Mary Oliver

We come full circle to Dante Alighieri who found himself lost in the dark wood in an existential crisis.

But he had Virgil to guide him on his journey into hell.

He was searching for God, for his love Beatrice, for himself. Through his travels and travails, he found what he was searching for.

I believe this journey is about rediscovering and reaffirming yourself again and again, in your heart and in your life, as you continually step into and embrace the unknown.

May you to reflect on all the moments you have said yes to your dreams, to something that called you, something that nudged you, something you wanted to do and somehow you did.

Even though you said to yourself, *I don't know what I'm doing.* You went ahead anyway. You said yes.

I ask you now: *What are you searching for? What is calling you?*

What is the truth that lives inside of you waiting to be expressed?

What is the dream you simply must say yes to?

Postscript

The artist, Grace, in Chapter One experienced a success disaster by replicating what worked. She finally realized that repeating herself in her art was a dead end. By experimenting and accessing the adjacent possible, she evolved as an artist.

At her most recent solo exhibition, Cannus showed up. She looked at him warily.

His eyes twinkling, he said, *I wouldn't miss this for the world.*

About The Author

Nancy Hillis, M.D. is a Stanford educated existential psychiatrist, abstract artist, speaker, founder of *The Artist's Journey* retreats and workshops and best-selling author of the award-winning book *The Artist's Journey: Bold Strokes To Spark Creativity*, named one of the Top 100 Creativity Books of all time by *BookAuthority* and winning the *Reader's Favorite* International Book Award Silver Medal. She has been featured in *Inc.* and *The New York Post.* You can find her at www.artistsjourney.com.

Other Books by Nancy Hillis, M.D.

**The Artist's Journey: Bold Strokes
To Spark Creativity**

A psychological and philosophical exhortation to trust
yourself and say YES to your deepest dreams. A "why-to",
not a "how-to" book to unleash your creativity and express
your deepest, most experimental art.

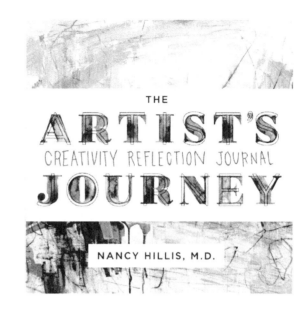

The Artist's Journey: Creativity Reflection Journal

Creativity is central to feeling alive. From the best-selling author of *The Artist's Journey: Bold Strokes To Spark Creativity*, a playfully illustrated inspirational self-help journal crafted to activate the inner sources of your creativity and the outer reaches of your imagination. Spark your imagination with prompts, poetic musings and stories inviting you to reflect on and activate the inner sources of your creativity.

Made in the USA
Coppell, TX
04 December 2022

87791396R00129